# AAT

## Synoptic Assessment
### Level 4
### Professional Diploma
### in Accounting
## Question Bank

Sixth edition 2021

ISBN 9781 5097 3936 3

Previous ISBN 9781 5097 3311 8

**British Library Cataloguing-in-Publication Data**

A catalogue record for this book is available from the British Library

**Published by**

BPP Learning Media Ltd
BPP House, Aldine Place
142-144 Uxbridge Road
London W12 8AA

www.bpp.com/learningmedia

Printed in the United Kingdom

Your learning materials, published by BPP Learning Media Ltd, are printed on paper obtained from traceable sustainable sources.

BPP
LEARNING MEDIA

# Contents

# Introduction

This is BPP Learning Media's AAT Question Bank for the *Professional Diploma in Accounting Level 4 Synoptic Assessment*. It is part of a suite of ground-breaking resources produced by BPP Learning Media for AAT assessments.

This Question Bank has been written in conjunction with the BPP Course Books and has been carefully designed to enable students to practise all of the relevant learning outcomes and assessment criteria for the units that make up the *Professional Diploma in Accounting Level 4 Synoptic Assessment*. It is fully up to date as at May 2021 and reflects both the AAT's qualification specification and the sample assessment provided by the AAT.

This Question Bank contains these key features:

- Tasks corresponding to each assessment objective in the qualification specification and related task in the synoptic assessment. Some tasks in this Question Bank are designed for learning purposes, others are of assessment standard.

- AAT's AQ2016 sample assessment 1 and answers for the *Professional Diploma in Accounting Level 4 Synoptic Assessment* and further BPP practice assessments.

The emphasis in all tasks and assessments is on the practical application of the skills acquired.

## VAT

You may find tasks throughout this Question Bank that need you to calculate or be aware of a rate of VAT. This is stated at 20% in these examples and questions.

## Test specification for the Level 4 synoptic assessment:

- Accounting Control and Systems (ASYC)
- Financial Statements of Limited Companies (FSLC)
- Management Accounting: Decision and Control (MDCL)
- Management Accounting: Budgeting (MABU)

| Assessment method | Marking type | Duration of assessment |
|---|---|---|
| Computer based assessment | Partially computer/partial human marked | 3 hours |

## Guidance from the AAT regarding completion of the Level 4 synoptic assessment

| | Assessment objectives for the Level 4 synoptic assessment | Weighting |
|---|---|---|
| 1 | Demonstrate an understanding of the relevance of the roles and responsibilities of the accounting function within an organisation and examine ways of preventing and detecting fraud and systemic weaknesses | 20% |
| 2 | Evaluate budgetary reporting and its effectiveness in controlling and improving organisational performance | 15% |
| 3 | Evaluate an organisation's accounting control systems and procedures | 15% |
| 4 | Analyse an organisation's decision making and control using management accounting tools | 15% |
| 5 | Analyse an organisation's decision making and control using ratio analysis | 20% |
| 6 | Analyse the internal controls of an organisation and make recommendations | 15% |
| **Total** | | **100%** |

# Approaching the assessment

When you sit the assessment it is very important that you follow the on-screen instructions. This means you need to carefully read the instructions, both on the introduction screens and during specific tasks.

When you access the assessment you should be presented with an introductory screen with information similar to that shown below (taken from the introductory screen from one of the AAT's AQ2016 sample assessments for the *Professional Diploma in Accounting Level 4 Synoptic Assessment*).

> We have provided this **sample assessment** to help you familiarise yourself with our e-assessment environment. It is designed to demonstrate as many of the question types that you may find in a live assessment as possible. It is not designed to be used on its own to determine whether you are ready for a live assessment.
>
> At the end of this sample assessment you will receive an immediate assessment result. This will only take into account your responses to tasks 1 and 5 as these are the elements of the assessment that are computer marked. In the live assessment, your reponses to tasks 2, 3, 4 and 6 will be human marked.

### Assessment information

- Read the scenario carefully before attempting the questions, you can return to it at any time by clicking on the 'Introduction' button at the bottom of the screen.

- Complete all 6 tasks.

- Answer the questions in the spaces provided. For tasks requiring extended written answers, the answer box will expand to fit your answer.

- You must use a full stop to indicate a decimal point. For example, write 100.57 **not** 100,57 or 100 57.

- Both minus signs and brackets can be used to indicate negative numbers **unless** task instructions say otherwise.

- You may use a comma to indicate a number in the thousands, but you don't have to.
  For example, 10000 and 10,000 are both acceptable.

- Where the date is relevant, it is given in the task data.

The actual instructions will vary depending on the assessment you are sitting. It is very important you read the instructions on the introductory screen and apply them in the assessment. You don't want to lose marks when you know the correct answer just because you have not entered it in the right format.

In general, the rules set out in the AAT sample assessments for this subject will apply in the real assessment, but you should carefully read the information on this screen again in the real assessment, just to make sure. This screen may also confirm the VAT rate used, if applicable.

A full stop is needed to indicate a decimal point. We would recommend using minus signs to indicate negative numbers (unless instructed otherwise by the task) and leaving out the comma signs to indicate thousands. This results in a lower number of key strokes and less margin for error when working under time

pressure. Having said that, you can use whatever is easiest for you as long as you operate within the rules set out for the assessment.

You have to show competence throughout the assessment and you should therefore complete all of the tasks. Don't leave questions unanswered.

In some assessments, written or complex tasks may be human marked. In this case you are given a blank space or table to enter your answer into. You are told in the assessments which tasks these are. **Note.** There may be none if all answers are marked by the computer. If these involve calculations, it is a good idea to decide in advance how you are going to lay out your answers to such tasks by practising answering them on a word document, and certainly you should try all such tasks in this Question Bank and in the AAT's environment using the sample assessment.

When asked to fill in tables, or gaps, never leave any blank even if you are unsure of the answer. Fill in your best estimate.

Note that for some assessments where there is a lot of scenario information or tables of data provided (eg budget information) you may need to access these via 'pop-ups'. Instructions will be provided on how you can bring up the necessary data during the assessment.

Take note of any task specific instructions once you are in the assessment. For example you may be asked to enter a date in a certain format or to enter a number to a certain number of decimal places.

Pay close attention to the language used in the question. Key words such as 'evaluate', 'justify', 'compare' and 'explain' will be key to answering the question in the most appropriate manner. The AAT website has a useful 'Writing Skills' presentation and quiz (www.aat.org.uk/learning-portal) which will introduce you to the various terms used, and help to give you guidance on your writing technique.

If an extended written task involves calculations, it is a good idea to decide in advance how you are going to lay out your answers to such tasks by practising answering them in a Word document. You should attempt all such tasks in this Question Bank and in the AAT's environment using the sample assessments.

When asked to fill in tables, or gaps, never leave any answers blank even if you are unsure of the answer. Fill in your best estimate.

AAT makes pre-release material about the scenario in this synoptic assessment available for you to read before you sit it. This will be available on the AAT website (student login required) at www.aat.org.uk/learning-portal (refer to Accounting Qualifications 2016/Professional Diploma Synoptic Assessment (AQ2016).

During the assessment you can access this pre-release material, plus other relevant information provided within the assessment, via 'pop-up windows'. Instructions will be provided on how you can bring up the necessary information during the assessment. For instance in one of the AAT sample assessments the following instructions are given:

---

**Scenario and pre-release material**

The real live scenario will be available on the AAT website. Please note, it will **not** be the same as the scenario in the sample assessment.

**Pop-ups**

The pre-release material is made available in every task via pop-up windows which can be opened by clicking on the links on the menu provided.

Other relevant reference material is shown in pop-up windows throughout the assessment. You can open these pop-up windows at any point by clicking on buttons that look like this:

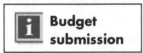

You can open, close and re-open the pop-ups as often as you want and you can position them anywhere on the screen.

Finally, take note of any task specific instructions once you are in the assessment. For example you may be asked to enter a date in a certain format or to enter a number to a certain number of decimal places.

---

## Grading

To achieve the qualification and to be awarded a grade, you must pass all the mandatory unit assessments, all optional unit assessments (where applicable) and the synoptic assessment.

The AAT Level 4 Professional Diploma in Accounting will be awarded a grade. This grade will be based on performance across the qualification. Unit assessments and synoptic assessments are not individually graded. These assessments are given a mark that is used in calculating the overall grade.

### How overall grade is determined

You will be awarded an overall qualification grade (Distinction, Merit, and Pass). If you do not achieve the qualification you will not receive a qualification certificate, and the grade will be shown as unclassified.

The marks of each assessment will be converted into a percentage mark and rounded up or down to the nearest whole number. This percentage mark is then weighted according to the weighting of the unit assessment or synoptic assessment within the qualification. The resulting weighted assessment percentages are combined to arrive at a percentage mark for the whole qualification.

| Grade definition | Percentage threshold |
|---|---|
| Distinction | 90–100% |
| Merit | 80–89% |
| Pass | 70–79% |
| Unclassified | 0–69% <br> Or failure to pass one or more assessment/s |

**Re-sits**

**The AAT Professional Diploma In Accounting is not subject to re-sit restrictions.**

You should only be entered for an assessment when you are well-prepared and you expect to pass the assessment. The AAT strongly recommend that you will have completed and been successful at the other units covered in this assessment PRIOR to sitting the final synoptic assessment.

## AAT qualifications

The material in this book may support the following AAT qualifications:

AAT Professional Diploma in Accounting Level 4, AAT Professional Diploma in Accounting at SCQF Level 8 and Certificate: Accounting (Level 5 AATSA).

## Supplements

From time to time we may need to publish supplementary materials to one of our titles. This can be for a variety of reasons, from a small change in the AAT unit guidance to new legislation coming into effect between editions.

You should check our supplements page regularly for anything that may affect your learning materials. All supplements are available free of charge on our supplements page on our website at:

www.bpp.com/learning-media/about/students

## Improving material and removing errors

There is a constant need to update and enhance our study materials in line with both regulatory changes and new insights into the assessments.

From our team of authors BPP appoints a subject expert to update and improve these materials for each new edition.

Their updated draft is subsequently technically checked by another author and from time to time non-technically checked by a proof reader.

We are very keen to remove as many numerical errors and narrative typos as we can but, given the volume of detailed information being changed in a short space of time, we know that a few errors will sometimes get through our net.

We apologise in advance for any inconvenience that an error might cause. We continue to look for new ways to improve these study materials and would welcome your suggestions. If you have any comments about this book, the BPP author of this edition can be emailed at: learningmedia@bpp.com

# Question Bank

# Chapter 1 – The accounting function: Accounting Systems and Controls

## Task 1.1

Johnson Services Ltd (JSL) is a large company which provides marketing services to small businesses. Each branch performs all its own accounting on a stand-alone laptop and emails results to the two directors once a month. The company has grown quickly and the directors are now concerned that its accounting function and systems are failing to support the business fully. They have approached you for some guidance.

(a) **Complete the following statement that you make to the directors.**

If you want your accounting system to be integrated then you need to

**(1)** [ ▼ ]. A key benefit of integrating the company's accounting system is that you can ensure every area of the business complies with relevant **(2)** [ ▼ ] .

**Picklist (1):**

centralise it
decentralise it

**Picklist (2):**

laws and regulations
operational objectives

(b) **For each of the following criteria, identify whether a centralised or a decentralised accounting function is better for JSL.**

| Criterion | Centralised accounting function ✓ | Decentralised accounting function ✓ |
|---|---|---|
| More economies of scope | | |
| Better communication with business units | | |
| Better placed to produce group accounts | | |
| More economies of scale | | |

## Task 1.2

**For each of the following tasks, identify which person will be responsible for their completion.**

| Task | Responsible party | |
|---|---|---|
| Preparation of budgetary control reports | | ▼ |
| Maintain accounting ledgers | | ▼ |
| Cash management | | ▼ |

**Picklist:**

Financial accountant
Management accountant
Treasury manager

## Task 1.3

**For each of the following parties, identify their responsibility within a limited company.**

| Party | Responsibility | |
|---|---|---|
| External auditors | | ▼ |
| Accounting function | | ▼ |
| Directors | | ▼ |

**Picklist:**

Maintain the accounting system
Prepare financial statements for the company
Report whether the financial statements show a true and fair view

## Task 1.4

The directors of JSL have decided to have a centralised accounting system with the accounting function operating from its headquarters building. They have identified a number of possible candidates for the role of chief accountant but each candidate has different levels of experience and qualifications. JSL's directors have approached you seeking guidance on the ethical and professional qualities for which they should be looking in their chief accountant.

**(a)** **If JSL's chief accountant acts diligently they are complying with part of which professional principle?**

|  | ✓ |
|---|---|
| Professional behaviour | |
| Objectivity | |
| Professional competence and due care | |
| Integrity | |

One of JSL's directors takes you aside to tell you about a problem encountered by one of the accounting function's staff Kim, an AAT member. A supplier of JSL contacted Kim and asked her to give the supplier a list of JSL's customers so that it could send the customers a mailshot. In return the supplier offered Kim a trip to Disney World. The director only discovered this when Kim told him.

**(b)** **Answer the following questions.**

**Which of the fundamental principles is threatened for Kim by this offer?**

|  ▼ |
|---|

**Picklist:**

Confidentiality
Integrity
Professional competence and due care

**What action should Kim take?**

|  ▼ |
|---|

**Picklist:**

She can accept but must advise all the directors
She can accept but must have no further dealings with the supplier
She may reveal the information but must decline the trip
She must refuse to reveal the information and decline the trip
She must resign from JSL

## Task 1.5

After identifying a variety of control activities for its accounting system, the chief accountant of JSL has raised a query about what type of security control each control activity represents. They are keen to ensure in particular that the passwords used within the accounting function are as strong as possible, but require further guidance on this.

**(a)** **For each of the following control activities used by JSL, identify what type of security control it is.**

| Control activity | Type of security control |
|---|---|
| Passwords | ▼ |
| Validation of input data | ▼ |
| Archiving | ▼ |

**Picklist:**

Access control
Integrity control
System control

**(b)** **Which of the following is the most secure password for use by JSL's accounting function?**

| | ✓ |
|---|---|
| Mmmeee | |
| 82s09PQ# | |
| 1357abcd | |

# Task 1.6

Within JSL's accounting function, the duties of sales invoicing, sales ledger and credit control are separated from each other. The person responsible for credit control, Iqbal Hussein, discovers that two sales invoices have been raised in respect of the same sale. Both invoices have been recorded in the sales day book and posted to the general and sales ledgers.

**What is the correct action for Iqbal to take?**

| | ✓ |
|---|---|
| Reverse the duplicate entries and advise the sales ledger team of his action | |
| Inform the sales invoicing team of the error | |
| Report the error to the chief accountant | |
| Prepare a credit note and send it to the customer | |

## Task 1.7

**Iqbal has asked you to tell him whether the following errors would be detected by reconciling the sales ledger to the sales ledger control account.**

| Error | Detected by reconciliation? |
|---|---|
| A batch of purchase invoices posted to the sales ledger control account | ▼ |
| A pricing error in a sales invoice | ▼ |
| VAT on a sales invoice posted to insurance rather than the VAT control account | ▼ |
| A sales invoice posted to the wrong customer account | ▼ |
| A sales invoice credited to the customer's account | ▼ |

**Picklist:**

Yes
No

## Task 1.8

The chief accountant of JSL has informed you that the company is intending to reduce costs by streamlining the accounting function and reducing the number of staff. They are considering getting Iqbal to take over the sales invoicing and sales ledger functions, in addition to his responsibility for credit control.

**Critically comment on this suggestion.**

## Task 1.9

Star Supplies Ltd is a rapidly expanding family-run business based in South Lincolnshire, who supply local fresh fruit and vegetable boxes to over 150 retail customers in Cambridgeshire and Lincolnshire. The managing director, Elysia Parker, is considering the strategy of the business over the next five years. She has come to you for some advice.

'I have heard about companies having a mission statement. Please can you explain what this means? We are also looking at developing our business and have considered two alternative directions:

- Growing our own produce; we currently rely on a number of local farmers, but cannot always get what we need, so we are considering growing our own range of King Edward potatoes and heritage carrots.

- Using our delivery network to supply homemade pizzas to the local area.'

**Explain what a mission statement is, focusing on the three main elements it should have to be effective. Explain how a mission statement could be useful for future strategic planning, such as considering the expansion options for the business.**

## Task 1.10

Iqbal has noted that Tripot Ltd (TL), a customer of JSL, is slow in paying its outstanding debt to JSL. From conversations with staff at TL he suspects that TL is experiencing serious financial difficulties. Iqbal's friend, Josh Jones, is considering selling goods on credit to TL. Iqbal has told Josh that he suspects TL is experiencing financial difficulties and will be unable to pay him.

BPP
LEARNING MEDIA

**Identify and explain which of the ethical principles Iqbal has breached by this action.**

## Task 1.11

**Which THREE of the following statements are MOST likely to be found in a sustainability report of JSL**

|  | ✓ |
| --- | --- |
| A discussion of sales figures for the main three products of JSL | |
| Highlighting the employee volunteering opportunities from a team helping to re-turf a school football pitch | |
| Reporting on the recycling efforts within the office environment | |
| Reporting any incidents of money laundering and how the organisation seeks to change its controls going forward | |

# Chapter 2 – Budgetary reporting: Accounting Systems and Controls/Management Accounting: Budgeting/Management Accounting: Decision and Control

## Task 2.1

**Your colleague, Jas, has asked you to explain some budgetary terms to them. Briefly explain each term.**

**(a)  Budgetary slack**

**(b)  Goal congruence**

**(c)  Relevant costs**

## Task 2.2

**Budget submission**

You have prepared a draft raw materials budget for the coming year for Smidget and Widget Manufacturing (SWP). SWP has four factories across the north west of England, with each factory having a small administration unit which runs the financials and payroll for that site. The main accounting and budgetary process is undertaken at the head office in Southport.

Background information

- The production budget (units) has already been agreed.

- The production manager and purchasing manager have decided to switch to a new supplier.

- The quality of the material will be improved which should reduce wastage.

- The material price will increase.

- Supply should be more reliable which means that inventory can be reduced.

- You have been asked to recommend performance indicators to monitor material costs and to give advice about ownership of the budget.

| Draft raw materials budget | This year actual | Next year budget |
|---|---|---|
| Production (units) | 64,000 | 67,840 |
| Material per unit | 0.4 kg | 0.4 kg |
| Material loss (wastage) | 12.5% | 10% |
| **Material** | **kg** | **kg** |
| Required for production | 29,258 | 30,152 |
| Opening inventory | 1,300 | 1,242 |
| Closing inventory | 1,242 | 1,000 |
| Purchases | 29,200 | 29,910 |
| **Material purchases** | **£** | **£** |
| Price per kg | 4.80 | 5.04 |
| **Purchases** | **140,160** | **150,747** |

**Write an email to the budget committee of SWP, which:**

**(a) Suggests FOUR appropriate performance indicators (other than cost variances) to monitor raw material costs.**

**(b) Explains which of the planning assumptions are based on forecasts and why these are not totally within the production manager's control.**

**(c) Explains the issues in the budget that may indicate a lack of goal congruence between the purchasing manager and the production manager.**

**To:** SWP budget committee     **From:** Budget accountant
**Subject:** Draft raw materials budget     **Date:** XX/XX/XXXX

**(a)** **Performance indicators**

**(b)** **Forecasts**

**(c)** **Lack of goal congruence**

# Task 2.3

## Budget revision

You have submitted a draft operating budget to the SWP budget committee based on Scenario A.

The committee has asked you to budget for an alternative situation, Scenario B, and calculate the increase or decrease in expected profit.

### Assumptions in Scenario A

- Material and labour costs are variable.
- Depreciation is a stepped cost, increasing at every 10,000 units.
- There is an allowance for an energy price rise of 4%.

### Assumptions in Scenario B

- Increase the selling price by 5%.
- Reduce the sales volume by 10%.
- Revise the energy price rise to 6%.

**(a)  Complete the Scenario B column in the operating budget table and calculate the increase or decrease in profit.**

| Operating budget | Scenario A | Scenario B |
|---|---|---|
| Sales price (£ per unit) | 6.00 | 6.30 |
| Sales volume (units) | 84,000 | 75,600 |
| | £ | £ |
| Sales revenue | 504,000 | |
| | | |
| Costs | | |
| Material | 201,600 | |
| Labour | 226,800 | |
| Energy | 17,680 | |
| Depreciation | 8,100 | |
| Total | 454,180 | |
| | | |
| Gross profit | 49,820 | |
| Increase/(decrease) in gross profit | | |

BPP LEARNING MEDIA

The managing director has asked that you respond to his queries regarding the possibility of centralising the administration and financial departments across the business.

**(b)** **Evaluate the effects on SWP of the impact of centralisation, specifically in terms of the financial, controls environment and decision-making factors.**

........................................................................................

## Task 2.4

**You are required to complete the monthly operating report below. Flex the budget, calculate variances and show whether each variance is favourable or adverse. The original budget and actual results have been entered.**

Notes.

1    Material, labour and distribution costs are variable.

2    Energy cost is semi-variable. The fixed element is budgeted at £12,800 per month.

3    Equipment hire is a stepped cost, budgeted to increase at every 30,000 units of monthly production.

4    Depreciation, marketing and administration costs are fixed.

## Monthly operating report

| Original budget | | Flexed budget | Actual | Variance Fav/(Adv) |
|---|---|---|---|---|
| 178,000 | Sales volume (units) | | 192,000 | |
| £ | | £ | £ | £ |
| 1,281,600 | Sales revenue | | 1,377,000 | |
| | Costs | | | |
| 462,800 | Materials | | 500,100 | |
| 480,600 | Labour | | 516,500 | |
| 67,640 | Distribution | | 74,200 | |
| 60,860 | Energy | | 65,080 | |
| 24,000 | Equipment hire | | 28,600 | |
| 8,800 | Depreciation | | 8,700 | |
| 78,000 | Marketing | | 78,900 | |
| 25,600 | Administration | | 24,820 | |
| 1,208,300 | Total | | 1,296,900 | |
| | | | | |
| 73,300 | Operating profit/(loss) | | 80,100 | |

## Task 2.5

### Operational review

Review the operating statement shown and the additional information below, and prepare a report by email.

### Additional information

The budget has been flexed to the actual number of units produced and sold. The original budget was based on an expected sales volume of 165,000 units which was expected to generate a profit of £227,000.

Sales volume reduced when a competitor undercut our prices. We responded with a 10% price reduction part-way through the year and expected to win back most of the volume in due course.

The budget allowed for a significant amount of overtime working but this was not required when sales volume fell. Material usage efficiency was better than expected and a budgeted increase in material price did not occur.

The original budget was prepared by a management committee and approved by the chief executive. She is concerned that profit is lower than originally budgeted and asks you how she can encourage the management team to perform better.

| Operating statement | Flexed Budget | Actual | Variance Fav/Adv |
|---|---|---|---|
| Sales volume | | 147,000 units | |
| | £000 | £000 | £000 |
| Sales revenue | 764 | 735 | (29) |
| Variable costs | | | |
| Material | 221 | 212 | 9 |
| Labour | 125 | 110 | 15 |
| Distribution | 25 | 24 | 1 |
| Power | 9 | 9 | – |
| Equipment hire | 138 | 132 | 6 |
| Total | 518 | 487 | 31 |
| Contribution | 246 | 248 | 2 |
| Fixed costs | | | |
| Power | 15 | 14 | 1 |
| Depreciation | 16 | 17 | (1) |
| Marketing | 12 | 11 | 1 |
| Administration | 7 | 8 | (1) |
| Total | 50 | 50 | – |
| Operating profit | 196 | 198 | 2 |

Write an email to the chief executive, in three parts, in which you explain:

(a)   The main reasons for the sales revenue, material and labour variances from the flexed budget, and how the sales revenue variance might have been avoided.

(b)   How to set and manage a budget to drive improved performance.

(c)   How the introduction of standard costing could assist effective budgetary control.

**To:**  The chief executive   **From:**  Budget accountant

**Subject:**  Review of operating statement   **Date:**  XX/XX/XXXX

(a)   **Reasons for variances**

**(b)    Setting and managing the budget**

**(c)    Standard costing**

## Task 2.6

### Costing queries

Your firm, Ridges Consulting, has been hired by entrepreneur Jack Hamilton, CEO of Hamilton Products Ltd (HPL). Jack does not have a background in accounting and has found himself at a loss to understand certain costing techniques.

**Answer the following query from Jack:**

**What difference does it make to profit if I use fewer subcontractors and hire more employees, thereby increasing fixed costs but reducing variable costs?**

## Task 2.7

### Limiting factors

Jack Hamilton has emailed you the following: 'I've just discovered that a material which is used in three of our products is likely to be in short supply for the foreseeable future. Since we're only likely to be able to get hold of 80% of what we need, I presume we just cut our production of all products by 20%?'

BPP
LEARNING MEDIA

**Reply to Jack**

---

## Task 2.8

### Pricing

Jack Hamilton has called you and asked the following: 'We've just been contacted by a company which is not normally one of our customers. They want us to quote a price for them to buy a substantial quantity of one of our products as a one-off order. We have sufficient production capacity to be able to do this. I'm just not sure of the price we should charge. The variable cost of the product is £187 per unit, the total cost is £279 per unit, and we normally charge £400 per unit. However, if we charge £400 I don't think we'd get the contract.'

**Advise Jack on the factors he should consider in determining the price.**

# Chapter 3 – Accounting control systems and procedures: Accounting Systems and Controls

## Task 3.1

**Complete the following statement:**

Allocating a payment from one customer to another customer's account in order to balance the books and detract from a shortfall is called [          ▼ ] .

**Picklist:**

identity fraud
inflation
reconciliation and review
teeming and lading

## Task 3.2

**Which of the following are the THREE types of fraud specified in the Fraud Act 2006?**

|  | ✓ |
|---|---|
| False representation | ✓ |
| Failure to segregate duties | ✓ |
| Failure to disclose information | ✓ |
| Abuse of position | |
| Duress and undue influence | |

## Task 3.3

Identify what, if any, effect each of the following systemic weaknesses in an accounting system will have on reported profit.

| Systemic weakness | Understatement of reported profit ✓ | Overstatement of reported profit ✓ |
|---|---|---|
| Overvaluation of inventory at the period end | | |
| Creating an unnecessary allowance for doubtful debts | | |
| Fictitious sales | | |
| Not writing off irrecoverable debts | | |
| Overstating expenses | | |

## Task 3.4

Identify whether each of the following systemic weaknesses in an accounting system could lead to misappropriation of assets and/or misstatement in the financial statements.

| Systemic weakness | Misappropriation of assets ✓ | Misstatement in the financial statements ✓ |
|---|---|---|
| Leaving offices where computers are held unlocked | | |
| Failing to maintain an asset register | | |
| Omitting inventory from the annual physical count | | |
| Creating a fictitious employee on the payroll | | |
| Failing to chase unpaid debts | | |

## Task 3.5

**Complete the following statement:**

Segregation of duties is a type of [                    ▼] over fraud in the accounting system.

**Picklist:**

application control
management control
physical control
staff control

....................................................................................

## Task 3.6

You have been asked to review the adequacy of the control in Hansom Ltd's sales procedures. Your review has established the following information.

The company operates an integrated accounting system which includes a sales accounting module. The sales manager is responsible for managing sales activities.

**Ordering and despatch:**

* All sales, except those for cash, must be documented on an official customer order. The order should state the agreed price, if known.

* Customer orders must be reviewed and signed by the sales manager.

* Large orders must be signed by the finance director.

* Five copies of the order form are printed. Once signed, the original is sent to the customer as an acknowledgement. A copy printed on yellow paper is sent to the accounts receivable clerk. A pink copy is sent to production and a green copy is sent to despatch. The orange copy is retained by the individual who took the order.

* When the goods are completed, production signs the pink copy and sends it to despatch.

* When the goods are sent out, despatch signs the green copy and sends it, with the pink copy, to the accounts receivable clerk.

**New customers:**

* New customers are contacted by the sales manager. She asks for a trade reference and banking details, and offers credit terms.

* She usually offers credit terms as either of the following:
    – One month from the end of the month in which delivery takes place
    – A 5% discount for payment within 21 days of delivery

    However, terms are subject to negotiation.

## Accounting:

- All sales invoices are raised by the accounts receivable clerk. He matches yellow, pink and green copy orders and prepares the invoices for sending to the customer.

- He posts the invoices to the computerised accounting system.

- He answers queries from customers, issuing credit notes when appropriate.

- Most customers pay through the bankers automated clearing system (BACS). The accounts receivable clerk checks the bank account weekly and posts receipts to the ledger accounts.

**Identify as many systemic weaknesses in the company's internal controls for handling sales on credit as you can, and explain how each weakness that you have identified could create a problem for the company.**

**Note.** You are **not** required to make recommendations to change procedures.

| No. | Weakness | Potential problem |
|-----|----------|-------------------|
| 1 | | |
| 2 | | |
| 3 | | |
| 4 | | |
| 5 | | |
| 6 | | |
| 7 | | |
| 8 | | |
| 9 | | |
| 10 | | |

## Task 3.7

You have been asked to review the adequacy of the control in Hansom Ltd's payroll procedures. Your review has established the following information.

The company operates an integrated accounting system which includes a payroll accounting module. The accounts manager, based at the head office, is responsible for managing payroll activities. The payroll clerk, based at the factory, performs day-to-day payroll tasks.

The payroll clerk:

* Maintains standing data on employees
* Records each employee's hours at work where this information is relevant and available
* Calculates gross pay and deductions
* Prepares the wages control account
* Prepares the BACS payments each month to employees and HMRC
* Reconciles total pay and deductions in the wages control account

Once a month the accounts manager reviews total payroll cost against budget and investigates unexpected variances.

**Which THREE of the following types of control activity are weakest in Hansom Ltd's payroll system?**

| | ✓ |
|---|---|
| Physical controls | |
| Segregation of duties | |
| Management controls | |
| Supervisory controls | |
| Organisation | |
| Authorisation (approval) of transactions | |
| Arithmetic and bookkeeping checks | |
| Personnel controls | |

## Task 3.8

Insyst Furniture Ltd (IFL) has grown rapidly in the last two years since its formation and now has a forecast revenue of £10m. The CEO has asked for your advice on the purchases system, which she feels may not be adequate for this size of company.

You have been told the following:

(1)     When materials are required for production, the production manager sends a hand written note to the buying manager. The buying manager finds a suitable supplier and raises a purchase order. The purchase order is signed by the CEO;

(2)     Materials for production are received by the goods received department, who issue a sequentially numbered goods received note (GRN) and send a copy to the purchases ledger clerk. There is no system for recording receipt of other goods and services;

(3)     The purchases ledger clerk receives the purchase invoice, matches it with the goods received note and purchase order (if available). The CEO authorises the invoice for posting to the purchases ledger;

(4)     The purchases ledger clerk analyses the invoice and posts it to the purchase ledger;

(5)     The purchases ledger clerk prepares the cheques and remittances, and posts the cheques to the purchases ledger and cash book; and

(6)     The CEO signs the cheques, and the purchases ledger clerk sends the cheques and remittances to the suppliers.

**Identify SIX weaknesses in controls in IFL's purchases system and the implications of those weaknesses.**

| No. | Weakness | Potential problem |
|-----|----------|-------------------|
| 1   |          |                   |
| 2   |          |                   |
| 3   |          |                   |
| 4   |          |                   |
| 5   |          |                   |
| 6   |          |                   |

## Task 3.9

The CEO of TML has approached you for advice on its payroll system. The company has grown rapidly and now has over 200 employees. There are concerns that the payroll system may not be adequate.

You have obtained the following information:

(1) On Monday mornings each employee takes a blank time card from a pile and writes his or her name and number at the top. Each day of the week they record their starting and finishing times. The following Monday each department supervisor collects the cards and forwards them to the wages clerk.

(2) Personnel and wages records are maintained by the wages clerk. From the time cards he calculates the hours worked by each employee and enters them into a payroll program on the computer. This program, using data from personnel records as to wage rates and deductions, produces the weekly payroll and a payslip for each employee.

(3) The wages clerk prepares a cheque requisition for the total net pay for the week, which is sent to the company accountant together with a copy of the payroll. The accountant draws up the cheque, made payable to cash, and has it countersigned by a director. The wages clerk takes the cheque to the bank and uses the cash to prepare the wage packets. Wage packets are given to the department supervisors for distribution to the employees in their department as they see fit.

(4) There is no personnel department. Each department supervisor has the authority to engage new employees and to determine changes in wage rates with the verbal consent of a director.

**Identify SIX weaknesses in controls in TML's wages system and the implications of those weaknesses.**

| No. | Weakness | Potential problem |
|-----|----------|-------------------|
| 1 | | |
| 2 | | |
| 3 | | |
| 4 | | |
| 5 | | |
| 6 | | |

## Task 4.1

**Complete the following statement.**

The [      ▼ ] total variance may be analysed into expenditure, efficiency and capacity variances.

**Picklist:**

fixed overheads
labour
materials
variable overheads

## Task 4.2

Yombo Ltd makes the product X07. The standard and actual results for the month of June 20X1 are as follows.

|  | | Standard | | Actual |
|---|---|---|---|---|
| Production (units of X07) | | 14,000 | | 13,500 |
| Direct materials | 17,500 litres | £28,875 | 16,800 litres | £106,000 |
| Direct labour | 3,500 hours | £59,500 | 3,650 hours | £65,700 |
| Fixed overheads (absorbed on a unit basis) | | £77,000 | | £79,500 |
| Total | | £165,375 | | £251,200 |

**Complete the following statements:**

(a)  The standard quantity of labour per unit is [            ] minutes.

(b)  The standard quantity of materials needed to produce 13,500 units of X07 is [            ] litres.

(c)  The standard labour hours to produce 12,000 units of X07 is [            ] hours.

(d)  The standard labour cost to produce 13,500 units of X07 is
£ [            ].

**(e)** The standard overhead absorption rate per unit is £ [         ].

························································································

## Task 4.3

Statham Ltd purchases 3,700 kilograms of material at a cost of £10,915. The total material price variance is £1,665 adverse.

**(a)  Complete the following statement.**

The standard cost per kilogram is £ [         ].

Statham Ltd purchases and uses 200,000 litres of a different material at a cost of £0.55 per litre. The budgeted production was 22,000 units which requires 220,000 litres of material at a total standard cost of £132,000. The actual production was 19,000 units.

**(b)  Complete the following statement.**

The material usage variance is £ [         ] [         ▼].

**Picklist:**

adverse
favourable

Statham Ltd expects to produce 10,000 units of X using 6,000 hours of labour. The standard cost of labour is £15 per hour. The actual output was 12,000 units. 6,900 hours of labour were worked and 7,300 hours were paid at a total cost of £105,850.

**(c)  Complete the following statements.**

The total labour efficiency variance is £ [         ] [         ▼].

**Picklist:**

adverse
favourable

The idle time variance is £ [         ] [         ▼].

**Picklist:**

adverse
favourable

························································································

# Task 4.4

Bert Ltd manufactures product RPB. Bert Ltd operates a standard cost system in which production overheads are fixed and absorbed on a _unit basis._

The budgeted activity is for the production of 28,000 units at a total fixed production cost of £350,000. The actual volume of production was 30,000 units and the fixed overhead expenditure variance was £35,000 favourable.

**Complete the following statements.**

The fixed overhead volume variance is £ [        ] [        ▼].

**Picklist:**

adverse
favourable

The actual fixed production overheads incurred were £ [        ].

# Task 4.5

Randall Ltd manufactures product RTF. The budgeted activity and actual results for the month are as follows.

|  | Budget | Actual |
|---|---|---|
| Production units (RTF) | 64,000 | 67,000 |
| Direct labour costs | £5,760,000 | £5,896,000 |
| Fixed overheads | £3,840,000 | £3,950,000 |

Overheads are absorbed on a labour hour basis and the budget uses 480,000 labour hours. The actual labour hours used to produce 67,000 units totalled 536,000 labour hours.

**Calculate the following variances.**

| Variance | Amount £ | Adverse/Favourable |
|---|---|---|
| Fixed overhead capacity |  | [        ▼] |
| Fixed overhead efficiency |  | [        ▼] |

**Picklist:**

adverse
favourable

## Task 4.6

The following budgetary control report has been provided for Pelling Ltd together with the variances calculated below.

| | Budget | | Actual | |
|---|---|---|---|---|
| Production (units) | | 12,400 | | 13,600 |
| Direct materials | 37,200 kg | £130,200 | 37,400 kg | £112,200 |
| Direct labour | 24,800 hours | £223,200 | 28,560 hours | £285,600 |
| Fixed overheads | | £234,000 | | £221,000 |
| Total cost | | £587,400 | | £618,800 |

| Variance | Amount ✓ |
|---|---|
| Direct materials price | 18,700 F |
| Direct materials usage | 11,900 F |
| Direct labour rate | 28,560 A |
| Direct labour efficiency | Not yet calculated |
| Fixed overhead expenditure | Not yet calculated |

Pelling Ltd normally prepares an operating statement under standard absorption costing principles but the financial director has asked you to prepare one under standard marginal costing principles.

**Place each variance into the correct column (favourable or adverse) and complete the table.**

| | | | £ |
|---|---|---|---|
| Budgeted variable cost for actual production | | | |
| Budgeted fixed cost | | | |
| Total budgeted cost for actual production | | | |
| **Variance** | **Favourable £** | **Adverse £** | |
| Direct materials price | | | |
| Direct materials usage | | | |
| Direct labour rate | | | |
| Direct labour efficiency | | | |
| Fixed overhead expenditure | | | |
| Fixed overhead volume | ▼ | ▼ | |
| Total variance | | | |
| Actual cost of actual production | | | |

**Picklist:**

22,645
N/A

........................................................................................

## Task 4.7

Keta Ltd operates a standard costing system and uses raw material C2X, which is a global commodity. The standard price was set based upon a market price of £450 per litre when the material price index for C2X was 120.50. The following information has been gathered:

- The price index increased to 126.525 in June 20X3.
- The raw material price variance for June was £375,000 adverse.
- 12,500 litres of material C2X were purchased in June.

**Complete the statements below. In order to calculate your answers, you should split the raw material price variance into two components by calculating the part of the variance explained by the change in the price index and the part of the variance not explained by the change in the price index.**

**(a)** The part of the variance explained by the increase in the price index is

£ [         ] .

**(b)** The part of the variance not explained by the increase in the price index is

£ [         ] .

**(c)** The percentage increase in the index is [         ] %.

Keta Ltd also uses product Z4QX and has collected data from the last few months in order to forecast the cost per kilogram of Z4QX in the next period.

|  | April 20X3 | May 20X3 | June 20X3 |
|---|---|---|---|
| Cost per kilogram of Z4QX (£) | 1,457.92 | 1,593.66 | 1,729.40 |

**(d)** **Complete the table below to forecast the expected price of product Z4QX in September and December 20X3.**

|  | September 20X3 | December 20X3 |
|---|---|---|
| Cost per kilogram of Z4QX (£) |  |  |

A colleague has calculated the least squares regression line (the line of best fit) for a different product as **y = 24.69 + 2.14x**, where y is the cost per kilogram (in £) and x is the monthly period. June 20X3 is period 41.

**(e)** **Complete the statement below.**

The forecast cost per kilogram, using the regression line, for September 20X3 is £ [         ] .

●●●●●●●●●●●●●●●●●●●●●●●●●●●●●●●●●●●●●●●●●●●●●●●●●●●●●●●●●●●●●●●●●●●●●●●●●●●●

BPP
LEARNING MEDIA

# Task 4.8

You have been provided with the following information for Vocco Ltd, which manufactures a product called Becks, for the month just ended.

|  | Budget | | Actual | |
|---|---|---|---|---|
| Production (units) |  | 20,000 |  | 21,000 |
| Direct materials | 80,000 kg | £880,000 | 83,000 kg | £954,500 |

The finance director has asked you to write a note to help in the training of a junior accounting technician. The notes are to explain the calculation of the total direct material variance and how this variance can be split into a price variance and a usage variance.

**Prepare a note explaining the total direct material variance and how it can be split into a price variance and usage variance. Calculations should be used to illustrate the explanation.**

# Task 4.9

You have been provided with the following information for two scenarios involving a company which operates an absorption costing system.

|  | Scenario 1 | Scenario 2 |
|---|---|---|
| Sales volume (units) | 120,000 | 150,000 |
|  | £ | £ |
| Revenue | 1,680,000 | 1,800,000 |
| Gross profit | 600,000 | 450,000 |
| Profit from operations | 275,000 | 200,000 |
| Capital employed | 2,298,400 | 2,100,340 |
| Inventory | 147,950 | 167,500 |

**(a)** **Calculate the following performance indicators for Scenario 1 and 2.**

|  | Scenario 1 | Scenario 2 |
|---|---|---|
| Return on capital employed |  |  |
| Inventory holding period in days |  |  |
| Sales price per unit |  |  |
| Full production cost per unit |  |  |

**(b)** **Complete the table below for Scenario 3.**

|  | Scenario 3 |
|---|---|
| Capital employed (£) | 175,000 |
| Return on capital employed (%) | 13 |
| Profit margin (%) | 14 |
| Gearing (%) | 32.75 |
| Profit (to the nearest £) |  |
| Sales revenue (to the nearest £) |  |

(c) **Fill in the boxes with the appropriate options to show how to calculate the gearing. If there is more than one correct answer, either answer will achieve full marks.**

**Options:**

| | | |
|---|---|---|
| Total non-current liabilities | Profit | 365 |
| Capital employed | Total equity | 100 |
| Total non-current liabilities plus Total equity | Total non-current liabilities less Total equity | Revenue |

## Task 4.10

Alpha Ltd makes two products, Tig and Tag. The following information is available for the next month.

| | Product Tig £ per unit | Product Tag £ per unit |
|---|---|---|
| Selling price | 4,000 | 4,950 |
| Variable costs | | |
| Material cost (£400 per kilogram) | 2,400 | 3,000 |
| Labour cost | 400 | 600 |
| Total variable cost | 2,800 | 3,600 |

|  | Product Tig £ per unit | Product Tag £ per unit |
|---|---|---|
| Fixed costs |  |  |
| Production cost | 450 | 450 |
| Administration cost | 300 | 300 |
| Total fixed costs | 750 | 750 |
| Profit per unit | 450 | 600 |
|  |  |  |
| Monthly demand | 200 units | 300 units |

The materials are in short supply in the coming month and only 3,000 kilograms of material will be available from the existing supplier.

**(a)** **Complete the table below.**

|  | Product Tig £ | Product Tag £ |
|---|---|---|
| The contribution per unit is |  |  |
| The contribution per kilogram of materials is |  |  |

**(b)** **Complete the following statement.**

The optimal production order for products Tig and Tag is [ ▼ ].

**Picklist:**

Tag then Tig
Tig then Tag

**(c)** **Complete the table below for the optimal production mix.**

|  | Product Tig | Product Tag |
|---|---|---|
| Production in units |  |  |

**(d)** **Complete the table below for the total contribution for each product.**

|  | Product Tig £ | Product Tag £ |
|---|---|---|
| Total contribution |  |  |

Alpha Ltd has been approached by another materials supplier who can supply up to 500 kilograms of material at a cost per kilogram of £500. This is a premium of £100 above the normal cost per kilogram.

**(e)** **Complete the table below.**

| Should Alpha Ltd purchase the additional material? | Give a reason |
|---|---|
| **(1)** ▼ | **(2)** ▼ |

**Picklist (1):**

Yes
No

**Picklist (2):**

The additional cost per kilogram is greater than the contribution per kilogram

The additional cost per kilogram is greater than the contribution per unit

The additional cost per kilogram is less than the contribution per kilogram

The additional cost per kilogram is less than the contribution per unit

# Task 4.11

Alpha Ltd is considering designing a new product, product BPT, and will use target costing to arrive at the target cost of the product. You have been given the following information.

- The price at which the product will be sold has not yet been decided.

- It has been estimated that if the price is set at £40 the demand will be 500,000 units, and if the price is set at £50 the demand will be 430,000 units.

- The costs of production include fixed production costs of £8,500,000 which will give a production capacity of 500,000 units.

- In order to produce above this level the fixed costs will step up by £1,500,000.

- The required profit margin is 30%.

- The variable cost per unit is £13 for the production volume of 430,000 units.

- For production volume of 500,000 units the variable cost will be £12 per unit.

**(a)** **Complete the table for both levels of demand.**

|  | Sales price £40 | Sales price £50 |
|---|---|---|
| The target total production cost per unit |  |  |
| The target fixed production cost per unit |  |  |
| The target total fixed production cost |  |  |

**(b)** **Complete the following statement.**

Alpha should set the price at [        ▼] in order to achieve the target profit margin.

**Picklist:**

£40
£50

## Task 4.12

You have been provided with the following information for Beta Ltd.

**Current position**

The price is currently £22 per unit. At this price demand is 150,000 units each year. The advertising costs are currently £500,000 per year. The current factory can produce a maximum of 400,000 units per annum. The labour and material costs are the only variable costs.

**Proposed position**

The price will reduce to £18 per unit. Advertising costs will increase to £750,000 per year and it is expected that this will increase demand to 300,000 units per year. The factory will still be limited to 400,000 units per year. The labour and material costs are the only variable costs.

The forecast information for each scenario is shown below.

| Statement of profit or loss | Current position (actual) | Proposed position (forecast) |
|---|---|---|
| Sales price per unit | £22 | £18 |
| Sales volume | 150,000 | 300,000 |
| | £ | £ |
| **Revenue** | 3,300,000 | 5,400,000 |
| | | |
| Direct materials | 750,000 | 1,200,000 |
| Direct labour | 900,000 | 1,800,000 |
| Fixed production costs | 600,000 | 600,000 |
| Total cost of sales | 2,250,000 | 3,600,000 |
| Gross profit | 1,050,000 | 1,800,000 |
| Fixed advertising costs | 500,000 | 750,000 |
| Administration costs | 300,000 | 400,000 |
| **Profit** | 250,000 | 650,000 |
| | | |
| Material cost per unit | £5.00 | £4.00 |
| Labour cost per unit | £6.00 | £6.00 |
| Fixed production cost per unit | £4.00 | £2.00 |
| Fixed advertising cost per unit | £3.33 | £2.50 |
| Gross profit margin | 31.82% | 33.33% |
| Profit margin | 7.58% | 12.04% |
| Inventory of finished goods | £350,000 | |
| Trade receivables | £500,000 | |

**Draft a report for the finance director covering the following:**

(a) An explanation of why the gross profit margin for the proposed position is higher than the current position, referring to the following:

- Sales volume
- Materials cost
- Labour cost
- Fixed production costs

(b) An explanation of what is likely to happen to the current asset position of the business by considering the following:

- Inventory levels (include a prediction of inventory level based upon the current inventory holding period)

- Trade receivable levels (include a prediction of the level based upon current trade receivables collection period)

| | | | |
|---|---|---|---|
| **To:** | Finance director | **Subject:** | Variances |
| **From:** | Accounting technician | **Date:** | Today |

(a) **Sales volume**

<br><br><br><br><br><br><br><br>

**Materials cost**

<br><br><br><br><br><br><br><br><br>

**Labour cost**

**Fixed production costs**

**(b)   Inventory levels**

**Trade receivables levels**

## Task 4.13

Seismic Security Systems Ltd (SSSL) is a rapidly expanding company which sells security cameras to small and medium-sized businesses. The CEO, Teresa Maynot, has asked you to review the sales system, which she currently oversees, and suggest how it should be updated in light of the company's growth. She has provided you with the following information about the existing system:

Sales are made through a team of five sales staff. As they are thought to know the customers best, they are responsible for assessing the creditworthiness of new customers and setting their initial credit limit. Sales staff are also able to make decisions on the amount of sales discount to grant to customers, up to a maximum of 20%, which they then record in the customer's master file.

Sales staff then email the despatch and accounting departments to initiate the despatch and invoicing of the goods. The company's terms of sale are 30 days, and at the end of each month a list of outstanding receivables over 120 days are passed to the sales staff for them to follow up with the relevant customers.

**(a)** **Suggest TWO new roles which SSSL should recruit in order to improve the sales system. Identify for each role the tasks they should take over and why.**

**(b)** **Explain TWO potential problems which SSSL might face after recruiting individuals to these roles.**

## Task 4.14

Gritby Fish Co manufactures three products – Prawn, Roe and Bass. The net profit from these is shown below:

|  | Prawn £ | Roe £ | Bass £ | Total £ |
|---|---|---|---|---|
| Sales | 100,000 | 80,000 | 120,000 | 300,000 |
| Variable costs | 60,000 | 50,000 | 70,000 | 180,000 |
| Contribution | 40,000 | 30,000 | 50,000 | 120,000 |
| Fixed costs | 34,000 | 36,000 | 40,000 | 110,000 |
| Profit/loss | 6,000 | (6,000) | 10,000 | 10,000 |

Gritby is concerned about the performance of Roe and is deciding whether it should cease production of them in order to produce a new product, Codlings.

The forecasted profit generated by Codlings is shown below:

|  | Codlings £ |
|---|---|
| Sales | 90,000 |
| Variable costs | 66,000 |
| Contribution | 24,000 |
| Fixed costs | 16,000 |
| Profit/loss | 8,000 |

Additional information

- The fixed costs associated with the production of Roe are £10,000.
- Directly attributable fixed costs of Codlings are £12,000.

**Critically appraise, using numerical evidence where appropriate, whether Gritby Fish Co should cease the production of Roe and start selling Codlings.**

●●●●●●●●●●●●●●●●●●●●●●●●●●●●●●●●●●●●●●●●●●●●●●●●●●●●●●●●●●●●●●●●●●●●●●●●●●●

# Task 4.15

Daisy Ltd owns two subsidiaries, Dandelion and Blossom.

Dandelion manufactures bespoke furniture, relying on local suppliers of sustainable wood and Blossom makes a mid-range equivalent, sourcing the raw materials from overseas. Both are sold to local, independent retailers, although customers do not buy from both companies, due to the different target audiences.

The forecasts for both factories for the year ending 31 December 20X5 are below:

| | Dandelion £000 | | Blossom £000 | |
|---|---|---|---|---|
| Revenue | 2,200 | | 2,850 | |
| Direct materials | 660 | | 784 | |
| Direct labour | 440 | | 448 | |
| Fixed production overheads | 220 | | 420 | |
| Cost of sales | 1,320 | | 1,652 | |
| Gross profit | 880 | 40% | 1,198 | 42% |
| Sales and distribution costs | 520 | | 640 | |
| Administration costs | 210 | | 250 | |
| Profit from operations | 150 | 6.8% | 308 | 10.8% |

Other information:

- Inventories are of raw materials and will remain unchanged throughout the year.
- All material and labour costs are variable.
- Sales and distribution costs are variable in proportion to the turnover from each factory.
- Administration costs are fixed.

The Managing Director has proposed closing Dandelion. The impact to Blossom's results will be as follows:

- Revenue would increase by 40%.
- Fixed production overheads will increase by £100,000.
- Administration costs will increase by £60,000.
- It is forecast that raw material purchasing costs will decrease by 5% as a result of the closure.

**(a)** **Prepare a revised statement of profit or loss for Blossom, assuming Dandelion is closed.**

|  | Blossom £000 |  |
| --- | --- | --- |
| Revenue |  |  |
| Materials |  |  |
| Direct labour |  |  |
| Fixed production overheads |  |  |
| Cost of sales |  |  |
| Gross profit |  | % |
| Sales and distribution costs |  |  |
| Administration costs |  |  |
| Profit from operations |  | % |

**(b)** **Recommend whether Dandelion should be closed or remain open, give brief reasons for your answer.**

**(c)** **Give ONE example of a non-financial consideration which the Board of Directors of Daisy Ltd should consider prior to making their decision. State a potential problem for the company relating to this consideration.**

## Task 4.16

Connolly Computers Ltd (CCL) develops and licences specialist computer software and hardware. CCL is experiencing increasing competition from rival companies, most of which specialise in hardware or software, but not both. There is pressure to advertise and to cut prices.

You have been provided with the following information:

### Statement of profit and loss

| | Year ended 31 Dec 20X3 £000 | Year ended 31 Dec 20X2 £000 |
|---|---|---|
| **Revenue** | 15,206 | 13,524 |
| Cost of sales | 3,009 | 3,007 |
| **Gross profit** | 12,197 | 10,517 |
| Distribution costs | 3,006 | 1,996 |
| Administrative expenses | 994 | 1,768 |
| Selling expenses | 3,002 | 274 |
| **Profit from operations** | 5,195 | 6,479 |
| Net interest receivable | 995 | 395 |
| **Profit before tax** | 6,190 | 6,874 |
| Income tax expense | 3,104 | 1,452 |
| **Net profit** | 3,086 | 5,422 |
| Retained profits | 1,617 | 3,983 |
| Dividends paid | 1,469 | 1,439 |
| | % | % |
| **Accounting ratios and percentages** | | |
| Gross profit percentage | 80 | 78 |
| **Expenses as a percentage of revenue** | | |
| Distribution costs | 20 | 15 |
| Administrative expenses | 7 | 13 |
| Selling expenses | 20 | 2 |
| Operating profit | 34 | 48 |

BPP LEARNING MEDIA

The following information is also available:

* In order to try and compete with their rivals, a new e-commerce portal to allow retail customers to buy direct from CCL was built at a cost of £350,000. This was launched in October 20X3.

* The Managing Director decided at the start of 20X3 to focus on sales, and made redundancies, mainly in the financial and customer support areas. New staff were recruited in the warehouse and sales teams, they were brought in quickly and told to 'go out and sell'.

* Budgets are drawn up once a year, and actuals are compared to budget. CCL does not flex its budgets once approved.

* The tax rate remains static year on year.

**(a)** **Evaluate whether the staff changes at CCL during 20X3 would have impacted upon the performance of the company. Identify any potential issues which may have arisen.**

**(b)** **Comment briefly on the financial performance of the company for the two years.**

# Chapter 5 – Ratio analysis: Accounting Systems and Controls/Financial Statements of Limited Companies/Management Accounting: Decision and Control

## Task 5.1

**Which of the following is the correct calculation of the working capital cycle?**

| | ✓ |
|---|---|
| Receivables days + Inventory days – Payables days | |
| Receivables days + Payables days – Inventory days | |
| Inventory days + Receivables days + Payables days | |
| Inventory days – Receivables days – Payables days | |

## Task 5.2

In accordance with the IASB Conceptual Framework for Financial Reporting:

**(a)** **Identify the TWO fundamental characteristics of useful information.**

| | ✓ |
|---|---|
| Understandability | |
| Relevance | |
| Comparability | |
| Faithful representation | |

**(b)** **Define the term 'income'.**

## Task 5.3

You have been given the financial statements of Bridport Ltd for the year ending 30 June 20X1. You are now required to prepare financial ratios to assist your manager in his analysis of the company.

Bridport Ltd's statement of profit or loss and statement of financial position are shown below.

**Bridport Ltd – Statement of profit or loss for the year ended 30 June 20X1**

|  | £000 |
|---|---|
| **Continuing operations** | |
| **Revenue** | 58,914 |
| Cost of sales | (42,126) |
| Gross profit | 16,788 |
| Distribution costs | (2,483) |
| Administrative expenses | (5,769) |
| **Profit from operations** | 8,536 |
| Finance costs | (1,642) |
| **Profit before tax** | 6,894 |
| Tax | (1,758) |
| **Profit for the year from continuing operations** | 5,136 |

**Bridport Ltd – Statement of financial position as at 30 June 20X1**

|  | £000 |
|---|---|
| **ASSETS** | |
| **Non-current assets** | |
| Property, plant and equipment | 42,792 |
| **Current assets** | |
| Inventories | 6,724 |
| Trade receivables | 5,278 |
| Cash and cash equivalents | 1,190 |
|  | 13,192 |
| **Total assets** | 55,984 |

| | £000 |
|---|---|
| **EQUITY AND LIABILITIES** | |
| **Equity** | |
| Ordinary share capital (£1 shares) | 16,000 |
| Retained earnings | 12,326 |
| **Total equity** | 28,326 |
| | |
| **Non-current liabilities** | |
| **Bank loans** | 20,400 |
| | 20,400 |
| **Current liabilities** | |
| Trade payables | 5,332 |
| Tax liabilities | 1,926 |
| | 7,258 |
| **Total liabilities** | 27,658 |
| **Total equity and liabilities** | 55,984 |

(a) Identify the formulae that are used to calculate each of the following ratios:

**Return on equity**

Picklist:

Profit after tax/Total equity × 100
Profit after tax/Total equity and liabilities × 100
Profit from operations/Total equity × 100
Profit from operations/Total equity and liabilities × 100

**Acid test ratio**

Picklist:

(Current assets – Inventories)/Current liabilities
Current assets/Current liabilities
Non-current liabilities/(Total equity + Non-current liabilities)
Total assets/Total liabilities

**Inventory holding period** [ ▼ ]

**Picklist:**

Cost of sales/Inventories
Inventories/Cost of sales × 365
Inventories/Revenue × 365
Revenue/Inventories

**Asset turnover (net assets)** [ ▼ ]

**Picklist:**

Profit from operations/(Total assets – Current liabilities)
Profit from operations/Total assets
Revenue/(Total assets – Current liabilities)
Revenue/Total assets

**Gearing** [ ▼ ]

**Picklist:**

Current assets/Current liabilities × 100
Non-current liabilities/(Total equity + Non-current liabilities) × 100
Profit from operations/(Total equity + Non-current liabilities) × 100
Revenue/(Total assets – Current liabilities) × 100

**(b) Calculate the above ratios to ONE decimal place**

Return on equity [ ] %

Acid test ratio [ ] : 1

Inventory holding period [ ] days

Asset turnover (net assets) [ ] times

Gearing [ ] %

# Task 5.4

Carol Bright, the Financial Director of Poole Ltd, is concerned that the company is not managing its working capital efficiently. She has asked for your assistance in identifying any problem area(s) and for your suggestions as to how these can be remedied.

You have calculated the following ratios in respect of Poole Ltd's latest financial statements and have also obtained each of their industry averages for comparative purposes.

| | Poole Ltd | Industry average |
|---|---|---|
| Current ratio | 5.1:1 | 2.3:1 |
| Inventory turnover | 7.2 times | 6.8 times |
| Trade receivables collection period | 63 days | 45 days |
| Trade payables payment period | 44 days | 51 days |

**Prepare a reply to Carol that includes:**

(a) **Comments on whether Poole Ltd has performed better or worse in respect of the calculated ratios, giving possible reasons, as compared to the industry averages.**

(b) **The steps to be taken to improve Poole Ltd's working capital cycle and any possible problems you think may arise from implementing these actions.**

## Task 5.5

Abbas Ltd uses a balanced scorecard to measure and control its financial performance. The Finance Director has asked you to calculate certain ratios for inclusion in the scorecard.

The following data is available.

| Extracts from accounts of Abbas Ltd | Year ended 31 December 20X4 £000 | Year ended 31 December 20X5 £000 |
|---|---|---|
| Revenue | 16,500 | 17,120 |
| Cost of sales | 7,540 | 8,480 |
| Gross profit | 8,960 | 8,640 |
| Profit from operations | 2,060 | 2,150 |
| **Assets** | | |
| Non-current assets | 5,780 | 5,060 |
| Inventories | 2,450 | 2,900 |
| Trade receivables | 1,870 | 2,010 |
| Cash and equivalents | 30 | 340 |
| **Total assets** | **10,130** | **10,310** |
| **Equity and liabilities** | | |
| Equity | 6,020 | 7,190 |
| Non-current liabilities | 2,590 | 1,070 |
| Trade payables | 1,130 | 1,670 |
| Tax liabilities | 390 | 380 |
| **Total equity and liabilities** | **10,130** | **10,310** |

(a) **Which TWO of the following statements are recommended perspectives in the Balanced Scorecard framework:**

| | ✓ |
|---|---|
| Financial perspectives of the company, such as profit margins | |
| Supplier perspectives, such as the number of supplier complaints | |
| Customer perspectives of the company, such as number of repeat orders | |

(b) **Complete the Balanced Scorecard by calculating the ratios for the year ended 31 December 20X5. Answers should be rounded to ONE decimal point, or whole days.**

| Abbas Ltd Balanced Scorecard | Year ended 31 Dec 20X4 | Year ended 31 Dec 20X5 |
|---|---|---|
| **Profitability and gearing (correct to 1 dp):** | | |
| Gross profit % | 54.3% | % |
| Operating profit % | 12.5% | % |
| Return on capital employed | 23.9% | % |
| Gearing (debt/debt + equity) | 30.1% | % |
| **Liquidity ratios (correct to 1 dp):** | | |
| Current ratio | 2.9:1 | :1 |
| Acid test/quick ratio | 1.3:1 | :1 |
| **Working capital days (correct to nearest day):** | | |
| Inventory holding period | 119 days | days |
| Trade receivables collection period | 41 days | days |
| Trade payables payment period | 55 days | days |
| Working capital cycle | 105 days | days |

**(c)** **Select the ONE correct observation about each aspect of business performance below.**

**(i)** **Profitability**

| | ✓ |
|---|---|
| This has been a year of steady, if unspectacular, progress. Although profitability has dipped, the return on capital employed has been kept under control. | |
| The profitability ratios give cause for concern. The small increase in sales revenue has not improved the gross profit percentage. Operating expenses have increased, reducing operating profit and return on capital employed. | |
| The ratios give mixed messages. Some have improved and some have deteriorated. Further investigation is required. | |

**(ii)** **Gearing**

| | ✓ |
|---|---|
| The decreased gearing ratio is due to the repayment of non-current liabilities. | |
| It is likely that the interest cover ratio has decreased. | |
| The increased gearing ratio shows that the company has become more risky. | |

**(iii)** **Liquidity**

| | ✓ |
|---|---|
| Both ratios have deteriorated which indicates that the company is less solvent than last year, however both ratios still fall within an acceptable level. | |
| Both ratios remain quite high, which may indicate that working capital is not being used effectively. | |
| Some liquidity ratios have improved and some have deteriorated. Further investigation is required to understand whether liquidity is improving. | |

## (iv) Working capital

| | ✓ |
|---|---|
| The working capital cycle has worsened. The inventory holding period has improved but the other ratios indicate a lack of financial control. | |
| There is a welcome improvement in the working capital cycle, mainly due to the change in the payment period for payables. | |
| The working capital cycle is worse than a year ago because of the increased revenue. | |

## (v) Overall performance

| | ✓ |
|---|---|
| Profitability has declined in 20X5. However, the gearing and liquidity measures show an improving financial position. | |
| 20X5 has been a bad year. Profitability has declined and finances are coming under pressure. | |
| Steady progress has been made in 20X5. The ratios show that the company is being better managed. | |

## Task 5.6

Explain the possible reasons for the following changes in the ratios of a company from one year to the next:

- An increase in the current ratio
- A decrease in the gross profit margin
- An increase in the inventory holding period
- An increase in gearing

**Note.** You are not required to show the calculation of the ratios.

····································································

## Task 5.7

**Answer the following questions with respect to ratio analysis.**

**(a)** An entity has an average gross profit margin of 23% and an average inventory turnover of 8 times, which is similar to the averages for the industry.

**The entity is likely to be:**

|  | ✓ |
|---|---|
| An architectural practice |  |
| A supermarket |  |
| An estate agent |  |
| A manufacturer |  |

**(b)** Extracts from the financial statements of Taurus are as follows:

| Statement of profit or loss | £000 |
|---|---|
| Operating profit | 230 |
| Finance costs | (15) |
| Profit before tax | 215 |
| Income tax | (15) |
| Profit for the year | 200 |

| Statement of financial position | £000 |
|---|---|
| Ordinary shares | 2,000 |
| Revaluation surplus | 300 |
| Retained earnings | 1,200 |
|  | 3,500 |
| 10% loan | 1,000 |
| Current liabilities | 100 |
| Total equity and liabilities | 4,600 |

### What is the return on capital employed?

|  | ✓ |
|---|---|
| 5.1% |  |
| 4.7% |  |
| 6.6% |  |
| 6% |  |

**(c)** Managing the operating cycle is an important part of managing working capital in a company.

**Which of the following will increase the length of a company's operating cycle?**

|  | ✓ |
|---|---|
| Reducing the receivables collection period |  |
| Reducing the inventory holding period |  |
| Reducing the payables payment period |  |
| Reducing time taken to produce goods |  |

**(d)** Analysis of the financial statements of Capricorn at 31 December 20X8 yields the following information.

| | |
|---|---|
| Gross profit margin | 30% |
| Current ratio | 2.14 |
| ROCE | 16.3% |
| Asset turnover | 4.19 |
| Inventory turnover | 13.9 |

**What is the operating profit margin?**

|  | ✓ |
|---|---|
| 3.9% |  |
| 7.6% |  |
| 16.1% |  |
| 7.1% |  |

## Task 5.8

Forrest Limited is considering an acquisition of either Peas Limited or Carrots Ltd, which both operate in the same industry. You have been provided with extracts from the financial statements of both companies for the year ended 31 December 20X7.

**Statements of profit and loss for the year ended 31 December 20X7**

|  | Peas £000 | Carrots £000 |
|---|---|---|
| Revenue | 12,000 | 20,500 |
| Cost of sales | (10,500) | (18,000) |
| Gross profit | 1,500 | 2,500 |
| Operating expenses | (240) | (500) |
| Finance costs | (210) | (600) |
| Profit before tax | 1,050 | 1,400 |
| Income tax expense | (150) | (400) |
| Profit for the year | 900 | 1,000 |
|  |  |  |
| **Note.** Dividends paid during the year. | 250 | 700 |

BPP LEARNING MEDIA

## Statements of financial position as at 31 December 20X7

| | Peas £000 | Carrots £000 |
|---|---|---|
| **Non-current assets** | | |
| Freehold factory | 2,600 | Nil |
| Plant and machinery | 5,000 | 7,400 |
| | 7,600 | 7,400 |
| **Current assets** | | |
| Inventory | 2,000 | 3,600 |
| Trade receivables | 2,400 | 3,700 |
| Bank | 600 | Nil |
| | 5,000 | 7,300 |
| **Total assets** | **12,600** | **14,700** |
| **Equity and liabilities** | | |
| Equity shares of £1 each | 2,000 | 2,000 |
| Revaluation reserve | 900 | Nil |
| Retained earnings | 2,600 | 800 |
| | 5,500 | 2,800 |
| **Non-current liabilities** | | |
| 7% loan notes | 3,000 | 3,200 |
| 10% loan notes | Nil | 3,000 |
| | 3,000 | 6,200 |
| **Current liabilities** | | |
| Bank overdraft | Nil | 1,700 |
| Trade payables | 3,100 | 3,800 |
| Government grants | 400 | Nil |
| Taxation | 600 | 200 |
| | 4,100 | 5,700 |
| **Total equity and liabilities** | **12,600** | **14,700** |

(a) **Calculate the following ratios for both companies, rounding off to ONE decimal place, or the nearest whole day:**

| | Peas | Carrots |
|---|---|---|
| Return on year-end capital employed (ROCE) | | |
| Gross profit margin | | |
| Operating profit margin | | |
| Current ratio | | |
| Closing inventory holding period | | |
| Trade receivables' collection period | | |
| Trade payables' payment period | | |
| Gearing | | |
| Interest cover | | |
| Dividend cover | | |

(b) **Critically appraise the relative performance and financial position of Peas and Carrots for the year ended 31 December 20X7, in light of the potential acquisition by Forrest.**

**Profitability**

**Gearing**

**Liquidity**

```

```

**Summary**

```

```

## Task 5.9

The most recent financial statements of Tiger Tea plc (TTP) are shown below:

**Statements of profit or loss for the year ended 31 December**

|  | 20X1 £000 | 20X0 £000 |
|---|---|---|
| Revenue | 25,500 | 17,250 |
| Cost of sales | (14,800) | (10,350) |
| Gross profit | 10,700 | 6,900 |
| Distribution costs | (2,700) | (1,850) |
| Administrative expenses | (2,100) | (1,450) |
| Profit from operations | 5,900 | 3,600 |
| Finance costs | (650) | (100) |
| Profit before taxation | 5,250 | 3,500 |
| Income tax expense | (2,250) | (1,000) |
| Profit for the year | 3,000 | 2,500 |

## Statements of financial position as at 31 December

|  | 20X1 £000 | 20X0 £000 |
|---|---|---|
| **ASSETS** | | |
| **Non-current assets** | | |
| Property, plant and equipment | 11,500 | 5,400 |
| Intangibles | 6,200 | Nil |
| | 17,700 | 5,400 |
| **Current assets** | | |
| Inventory | 3,600 | 1,800 |
| Trade receivables | 2,400 | 1,400 |
| Bank | Nil | 4,000 |
| | 6,000 | 7,200 |
| **TOTAL ASSETS** | **23,700** | **12,600** |
| **EQUITY AND LIABILITIES** | | |
| **Equity** | | |
| Equity shares of £1 each | 5,000 | 5,000 |
| Retained earnings | 4,500 | 2,250 |
| | 9,500 | 7,250 |
| **Non-current liabilities** | | |
| 5% loan notes | 2,000 | 2,000 |
| 8% loan notes | 7,000 | Nil |
| | 9,000 | 2,000 |
| **Current liabilities** | | |
| Bank overdraft | 200 | Nil |
| Trade payables | 2,800 | 2,150 |
| Current tax payable | 2,200 | 1,200 |
| | 5,200 | 3,350 |
| **TOTAL EQUITY AND LIABILITIES** | **23,700** | **12,600** |

(a) **Calculate the following ratios for each year, rounding off to ONE decimal place, or the nearest day.**

|  | 20X1 | 20X0 |
|---|---|---|
| Net profit % |  |  |
| Operating profit % |  |  |
| Gross profit % |  |  |
| ROCE |  |  |
| ROE |  |  |
| Gearing |  |  |
| Interest cover |  |  |
| Current ratio |  |  |
| Quick ratio |  |  |

(b) **Critically comment on the performance in 20X1 relative to 20X0 from the perspective of shareholders, under the following headings:**

**Profitability**

**Gearing**

**Liquidity**

# Chapter 6 – Internal controls: Accounting Systems and Controls/Financial Statements of Limited Companies/Management Accounting: Budgeting/Management Accounting: Decision and Control

## Task 6.1

To date Rees Ltd has paid its suppliers by cheque. Rees Ltd now plans to pay larger suppliers by BACS, extending this method to all suppliers in time.

**Complete the following statements.**

Rees Ltd's plan is [ ▼ ] change.

**Picklist:**

a transformational
an incremental

The fact that the time of Rees Ltd's accounting staff will be freed up by not having to complete cheques by hand is [ ▼ ].

**Picklist:**

a tangible benefit of the change
a tangible cost of the change
an intangible benefit of the change
an intangible cost of the change

## Task 6.2

You have been asked to identify some improvements to the controls in Sleeptight Ltd's sales ordering procedures.

- Sleeptight Ltd makes high-value bespoke wooden bedroom furniture to order.

- An official customer order is created for each sale by a sales executive. The order must state the product and agreed delivery date. It also states the approximate price.

- Customer orders must be reviewed and signed by the sales manager.

- Orders for more than three pieces of furniture for one customer must be signed by the sales director.

(a)   **Identify ONE strength in these procedures. Explain how the business benefits from this.**

(b)   **Identify ONE weakness in these procedures. Explain how this damages the business and suggest a remedy.**

(c)   **Identify an opportunity to improve the procedures. Explain how the procedure should be changed and how the business could benefit.**

# Task 6.3

You have been asked to suggest some improvements to the controls in Sleeptight Ltd's sales accounting procedures.

- Sleeptight Ltd makes high-value bespoke wooden bedroom furniture to order.

- The company operates an integrated accounting system which includes a sales accounting module. The sales manager is responsible for managing all sales activities.

- Before an order is taken from a new customer, the sales manager performs a credit check on them and obtains their banking details. The sales manager has the authority either to offer credit terms or to require payment by bank transfer before delivery of the furniture.

- Credit terms offered are always two months from the end of the month in which delivery takes place, with a 15% discount for payment within 10 days of delivery. Payment is required via bank transfer.

- All sales invoices are raised by the accounts receivable clerk, who produces the invoice by checking the despatch note to the customer order, then confirming the agreed price and terms with the sales manager.

- The accounts receivable clerk posts the invoices to the computerised accounting system, answers any queries from customers and issues credit notes when appropriate.

- The accounts receivable clerk checks the bank account weekly for bank transfers by customers and posts receipts to the ledger accounts.

**(a)** **Identify ONE strength in these procedures. Explain how the business benefits from this.**

**(b)** **Identify ONE weakness in these procedures. Explain how this damages the business and suggest a remedy.**

**(c)** **Identify an opportunity to improve the procedures. Explain how the procedure should be changed and how the business could benefit.**

## Task 6.4

You have been asked to suggest some improvements to the controls in Sleeptight Ltd's purchase ordering procedures.

* Sleeptight Ltd makes high-value bespoke wooden bedroom furniture to order.

* All purchases, except petty cash items, must be documented on an official purchase order. The order should state the agreed price, if known.

* All departments are provided with books of pre-numbered order forms. These books can be obtained from the stationery store.

* Orders for production materials must be signed by the production manager.

* Capital expenditure orders must be signed by the finance director.

- There is no cash limit for purchase orders provided that they are within the approved budget.

- Other orders must be signed by the relevant budget holders.

- New suppliers are given a trade reference by the purchasing manager, who also requests credit terms. These are subject to negotiation, though the company's preferred terms are to pay 60 days from the end of the month in which delivery takes place.

**(a)** **Identify ONE strength in these procedures. Explain how the business benefits from this.**

**(b)** **Identify the weaknesses in these procedures. Explain how each one damages the business and suggest a remedy.**

**(c)** **Identify an opportunity to improve the procedures. Explain how the procedure should be changed and how the business could benefit.**

## Task 6.5

You have been asked to suggest some improvements to the controls in Sleeptight Ltd's purchase accounting procedures.

* Sleeptight Ltd makes high-value bespoke wooden bedroom furniture to order.

* Four copies of each purchase order form are printed. Once signed, the original is sent to the supplier. A yellow copy is sent to the accounts payable clerk. A pink copy is retained by the individual who raised the order, while a green copy is sent to Goods Inwards.

* When the goods or service(s) are received, Goods Inwards checks the goods, signs the green copy and sends it to the accounts payable clerk.

* All purchase invoices received are checked by the accounts payable clerk, who checks the calculations, matches them to appropriate yellow and signed green copy orders and clears the invoices for payment.

* The accounts payable clerk posts the cleared invoices to the computerised accounting system and takes up queries with suppliers, requesting credit notes when appropriate.

* Invoices are automatically paid as they fall due through the bankers automated clearing system (BACS). The accounts payable clerk authorises one payment run every week.

* The accounts payable clerk is authorised to pay early if a discount of at least 5% is offered by the supplier.

**(a)** **Identify the strengths in these procedures. Explain how the business benefits from these.**

**(b)** **Identify ONE weakness in these procedures. Explain how this damages the business and suggest a remedy.**

. . . . . . . . . . . . . . . . . . . . . . . . . . . . . . . . . . . . . . . . . . . . . . . . . . . . . . . . . . . . . . . . . . . . . . . . . . . . . . . . . . . . . . . . . . . .

## Task 6.6

You have been asked to review the adequacy of the control in Sleeptight Ltd's payroll procedures.

The company operates an integrated accounting system which includes a payroll accounting module. The accounts manager, based at the head office, is responsible for managing payroll activities. The payroll clerk, based at the factory, performs day-to-day payroll tasks.

- Sleeptight Ltd makes high-value bespoke wooden bedroom furniture to order.

- Non-production staff are salaried and are not entitled to paid overtime.

- Production staff are all full-time. They are paid at time and a half their basic rate if they work more than 40 hours per week.

- Production staff sign themselves in and out of the factory each day, using the signing-in book which is kept in the staff locker room.

- Production staff record hours spent on individual items of bespoke furniture on job sheets that follow the items around the factory. These job sheets are checked and signed by production supervisors.

The payroll clerk:

- Maintains standing data on employees

- Calculates each employee's hours at work each week from the signing-in book

- Calculates gross pay and deductions for production staff weekly, and for other staff monthly

- Maintains the wages control account

- Prepares the bank payments each week/month to employees and HMRC

- Reconciles total pay and deductions in the wages control account

Once a month the accounts manager reviews total payroll cost against budget and investigates any large unexpected variances.

**(a)** **Identify ONE strength in these procedures. Explain how the business benefits from this.**

**(b)** Identify the weaknesses in these procedures. Explain how these damage the business and suggest remedies.

**(c)** Identify an opportunity to improve the procedures. Explain how the procedure should be changed and how the business could benefit.

## Task 6.7

A company wishes to avoid or reduce certain specific risks in each of its three main transaction streams.

**You are required to identify a control objective and control activity for each risk.**

| Transaction stream | Risk | Control objective | Control activity |
|---|---|---|---|
| Purchasing | Company pays for goods it does not receive | | |
| Sales | Sales recorded late so fines incurred from HMRC with respect to VAT | | |
| Payroll | Company overpays | | |

## Task 6.8

You are presented with the monthly operating report below. The original budget has been flexed to the level of actual activity, and variances calculated.

You are told that:

- Material, labour and distribution costs are variable.

- Energy cost is semi-variable. The fixed element is budgeted at £12,800 per month.

- Equipment hire is a stepped cost, budgeted to increase at every 30,000 units of monthly production.

- Depreciation, marketing and administration costs are fixed.

- The company does not use full absorption costing.

## Monthly operating report

| Original budget | | Flexed budget | Actual | Variance Fav/(Adv) |
|---|---|---|---|---|
| 178,000 | Sales volume (units) | | 192,000 | |
| £ | | £ | £ | £ |
| 1,281,600 | Sales revenue | 1,382,400 | 1,377,000 | –5,400 |
| | Costs | | | |
| 462,800 | Materials | 499,200 | 500,100 | –900 |
| 480,600 | Labour | 518,400 | 516,500 | 1,900 |
| 67,640 | Distribution | 72,960 | 74,200 | –1,240 |
| 60,860 | Energy | 64,640 | 65,080 | –440 |
| 24,000 | Equipment hire | 28,000 | 28,600 | –600 |
| 8,800 | Depreciation | 8,800 | 8,700 | 100 |
| 78,000 | Marketing | 78,000 | 78,900 | –900 |
| 25,600 | Administration | 25,600 | 24,820 | 780 |
| 1,208,300 | Total | 1,295,600 | 1,296,900 | –1,300 |
| | | | | |
| 73,300 | Operating profit/(loss) | 86,800 | 80,100 | –6,700 |

**Write an email to the chief executive to explain the following.**

(a)   **The main factors that led to the actual profit being higher than the original budgeted profit.**

(b)   **Whether improved internal controls might assist in controlling the adverse variances.**

## Task 6.9

A company wishes to avoid or reduce certain specific risks in each of its three main transaction streams.

**You are required to identify a control objective and control activity for each risk.**

| Transaction stream | Risk | Control objective | Control activity |
|---|---|---|---|
| Payroll | Company incurs fines from HMRC | | |
| Sales | Custom lost through chasing payments already made by the customer | | |
| Purchasing | Company pays the wrong supplier | | |

## Task 6.10

A firm of accountants, Crachett & Co has decided to train all new staff in basic bookkeeping as part of their induction programme.

**(a)** **Identify the costs of such a decision, explaining the terms 'tangible costs' and 'intangible costs' in your response.**

As part of the reorganisation of the firm of accountants, other areas of the business are being reviewed. Crachett & Co are also considering a new accountancy software, however, it is expensive and the partners are unsure about whether to commit to it.

A software company, MoneyWise has quoted Crachett & Co for their new system.

Dear Sirs

Thank you for your interest in our fully integrated Client Pro Systems accounting system. We are happy to provide you with details of the following:

- Client Pro System 1 (Cloud).

- Sales ledger system, including pre-numbered invoices and aged debt reports.

- Purchases ledger system, incorporating purchase orders which can be matched against incoming invoices. Inventory aging reports are included.

- General ledger and summary trial balance reports.

- Exception reporting.

- Financial reporting tool for multi-client usage, incorporating iXBRL tax information, bookkeeping interface and payroll facility.

- Updates and upgrades occur regularly and will be automated at no extra cost.

## Annual costs

|  | Initial costs | Annual costs |
|---|---|---|
| Client Pro system 1 (cloud) | £7,500 (to cover assistance with data migration) | £3,300 (up to 15 licensed users) |

Training costs for the new system would be:

In-house training (maximum of 15 people)     £2,700

Course at local college (1 day)     £275 per person

Online course (completed in own time)     £75 per person (access limited to 6 months)

If you have any further questions, please do not hesitate to contact us.

Yours sincerely

E.Scrooge

Sales Director
MoneyWise

**(b)** **Evaluate the proposed new software, considering the factors in a cost-benefit analysis.**

# Answer Bank

# Chapter 1 – The accounting function: Accounting Systems and Controls

## Task 1.1

**(a)**

If you want your accounting system to be integrated then you need to
[ centralise it ]. A key benefit of integrating the company's
accounting system is that you can ensure every area of the business
complies with relevant [ laws and regulations ].

**(b)**

| Criterion | Centralised accounting function ✓ | Decentralised accounting function ✓ |
|---|---|---|
| More economies of scope | ✓ | |
| Better communication with business units | | ✓ |
| Better placed to produce group accounts | ✓ | |
| More economies of scale | ✓ | |

## Task 1.2

| Task | Responsible party |
|---|---|
| Preparation of budgetary control reports | Management accountant |
| Maintain accounting ledgers | Financial accountant |
| Cash management | Treasury manager |

## Task 1.3

| Party | Responsibility |
|---|---|
| External auditors | Report whether the financial statements show a true and fair view |
| Accounting function | Maintain the accounting system |
| Directors | Prepare financial statements for the company |

## Task 1.4

**(a)**

| | ✓ |
|---|---|
| Professional behaviour | |
| Objectivity | |
| Professional competence and due care | ✓ |
| Integrity | |

**(b)**

| Confidentiality |
|---|

| She must refuse to reveal the information and decline the trip |
|---|

## Task 1.5

**(a)**

| Control activity | Type of security control |
|---|---|
| Passwords | Access control |
| Validation of input data | Integrity control |
| Archiving | System control |

**(b)**

|  | ✓ |
|---|---|
| Mmmeee |  |
| 82s09PQ# | ✓ |
| 1357abcd |  |

## Task 1.6

|  | ✓ |
|---|---|
| Reverse the duplicate entries and advise the sales ledger team of his action |  |
| Inform the sales invoicing team of the error | ✓ |
| Report the error to the chief accountant |  |
| Prepare a credit note and send it to the customer |  |

## Task 1.7

| Error | Detected by reconciliation? |
|---|---|
| A batch of purchase invoices posted to the sales ledger control account | Yes |
| A pricing error in a sales invoice | No |
| VAT on a sales invoice posted to insurance rather than the VAT control account | No |
| A sales invoice posted to the wrong customer account | No |
| A sales invoice credited to the customer's account | Yes |

## Task 1.8

The proposed action violates the principle of segregation of duties. This means that different people should be responsible for different parts of the accounting system to minimise the chance of fraud and error.

For example, if Iqbal were to perform all of these functions he could potentially steal cash received from a customer and cover it up by writing off the debt or issuing a credit note.

If Iqbal were to make errors in performing his duties, for example issuing the same invoice twice (as in Task 1.6), then the chances of it being detected are reduced if there are no other people involved. It is much easier to spot errors made by other people than to spot your own.

Finally, Iqbal could well become overburdened by his increased responsibilities. This is likely to lead to more errors and also a lack of efficiency in, for example, chasing customers for payment.

## Task 1.9

Mission statements are published for the benefit of employees and other stakeholders of the organisation, such as the customers and suppliers. There is no standard format, but mission statements should generally be:

- **Brief** – to help ensure they are easy to understand and remember
- **Flexible** – to help accommodate change
- **Distinctive** – to make the organisation stand out

Mission statements are useful as they allow management to refer to the core beliefs of the business. This is especially important if the company is considering moving into new business areas, such as Star Supplies growing their own produce or delivering fast food. By considering the mission statement, management can see whether the new ideas are a 'good fit' for the current business, or whether it may only add to confusion for the existing customer and supplier base.

## Task 1.10

Iqbal has breached the principle of confidentiality. He has gained information during the course of his employment and should not reveal that information to any unauthorised person, without the prior consent of all parties; nor should he use it for his own purposes.

Iqbal should not reveal the information to a third party and he should also not reveal the information to anyone within JSL who does not require the information by virtue of their duties. For example, it would be acceptable to reveal the information to the Chief Accountant but not to the payroll clerk.

Iqbal may also be considered to have breached the principle of professional behaviour, by spreading rumours about TL Ltd. Iqbal has no confirmed evidence that TL is, in fact, in financial difficulty.

## Task 1.11

|  | ✓ |
| --- | --- |
| A discussion of sales figures for the main three products of JSL |  |
| Highlighting the employee volunteering opportunities from a team helping to re-turf a school football pitch | ✓ |
| Reporting on the recycling efforts within the office environment | ✓ |
| Reporting any incidents of money laundering and how the organisation seeks to change its controls going forward | ✓ |

A sustainability report will look at any non-compliance with regulations (money laundering), any organisational efforts to reduce the environmental impact (recycling) and raising awareness of social responsibility (helping out a local school). The sales figures are more likely to be mentioned as part of performance within a director's report (if at all) to support any going concern worries by stakeholders, or more likely, to not be mentioned in any great detail in public financial statements.

# Chapter 2 – Budgetary reporting: Accounting Systems and Controls/Management Accounting: Budgeting/Management Accounting: Decision and Control

## Task 2.1

### (a) Budgetary slack

Budgetary slack is an extra amount of cost built into a budget by budget holders in order to make the targets easier to meet.

### (b) Goal congruence

Goal congruence is where the goals of individual functions or departments are consistent with the overall goals and strategy of the organisation. Therefore, supporting the budget co-ordination between departments, encouraging team working and aiming to reduce 'silo' thinking between them.

### (c) Relevant costs

A relevant cost (sometimes known as an avoidable cost) is a future, incremental cash flow arising as a direct consequence of a decision. Relevant costs are those costs that are changed by decision.

## Task 2.2

### (a) Performance indicators

A number of assumptions have been made in this budget and we need to monitor their achievement.

Raw material costs are variable and we should expect them to increase or decrease with production levels. I recommend that we review the following four indicators on a weekly basis.

- Material usage per unit of production
- Percentage of material wastage
- Price per kilogram
- Number of days of inventory held

Variations in any of these indicators will impact on overall materials cost, and so should be monitored closely.

## (b) Forecasts

Although the production manager should take ownership of this budget there are aspects of it which are not wholly within his control.

- Purchase prices will be negotiated by the purchasing manager. The two managers need to work together to balance quality with price.

- Wastage is an important factor and is at least partly dependent upon quality. The wastage level has been estimated for budget purposes and must be monitored carefully.

- A reduction in inventory is planned. This will only be sensible if the supplier proves to be more reliable, as anticipated.

- Finally, the production manager cannot control production demand, although allowance for this can be made with budget flexing.

## (c) Lack of goal congruence

The purchasing manager's performance will be assessed on his ability to acquire raw materials for the lowest possible unit cost and the production manager will be assessed on his ability to manage the production of finished goods at the lowest possible cost. This could lead to conflicts due to a lack of goal congruence in two main areas.

**(i)** Material usage:

The production manager will aim to use the least amount of raw materials to achieve budgeted production. However the purchasing manager is likely to be able to negotiate a lower price per kilogram if more kilograms are purchased.

**(ii)** Cost and quality:

The purchasing manager will want to acquire raw materials for the lowest possible cost, yet low cost materials might be of poor quality, which will impact on wastage levels and therefore materials usage. This will have adverse consequences for the production manager.

# Task 2.3

**(a)**

| Operating budget | Scenario A | Scenario B |
| --- | --- | --- |
| Sales price (£ per unit) | 6.00 | 6.30 |
| Sales volume (units) | 84,000 | 75,600 |

|  | £ | £ |
| --- | --- | --- |
| Sales revenue | 504,000 | 476,280 |
|  |  |  |
| Costs |  |  |
| Material | 201,600 | 181,440 |
| Labour | 226,800 | 204,120 |
| Energy | 17,680 | 18,020 |
| Depreciation | 8,100 | 7,200 |
| Total | 454,180 | 410,780 |
|  |  |  |
| Gross profit | 49,820 | 65,500 |
| Increase/(decrease) in gross profit |  | 15,680 |

### Workings

Sales price = £6.00 × 1.05 = £6.30

Sales volume = 84,000 × 90% = 75,600 units

Sales revenue = 75,600 × £6.30 = £476,280

Materials = £201,600 × 90% = £181,440

Labour = £226,800 × 90% = £204,120

Energy = £17,680 × 1.06/1.04 = £18,020

Depreciation = £8,100 × 8/9 = £7,200

### (b) Financial factors

The benefits of centralising the administrative and financial parts of the SWP business would result in efficiencies in terms of avoiding duplication of roles (a centrally based payroll team, rather than multiple teams in the local sites).

The potential drawbacks would involve short term higher costs due to potential redundancies of staff, relocation expenditure for retained staff, training costs to ensure consistencies of approach and capital expenditure to ensure the head office can house the increased staff with the necessary equipment.

## Control environment

By having a central team working on financial and administration tasks, all of the tasks are being completed by one team, which is easier and more controllable. The controls surrounding the completion of the financial records can be more closely monitored by management due to the proximity of the teams.

Month end and annual accounting processes should be more efficient, as different teams of accounts payable, accounts receivable, treasury etc can work together as they are in the same location.

There can be standardised and consistent procedures which are more easily controlled if the staff are in the same location. Different approaches or timescales are avoided.

More specialised knowledge can be held in one location, for example, human resources and payroll can be centralised on one site, allowing close working and timely interactions between the different disciplines.

However, the interim period once any announcement has been made to the company may result in low productivity of staff (the threat of redundancy or fear of the unknown), low morale and potentially poor levels of control especially from the local sites.

## Decision-making factors

Decisions can be made taking into account the whole company view, rather than relying on the potentially differing opinions of the site teams, which should lead to increased goal congruence.

Major decisions, such as capital expenditure, recruitment and training can be centrally debated and decided upon, making the process more efficient and arguably better informed as the results from all sites can be considered.

However, it is possible that analysis and decision making would become more remote from the operational centres, and a reduced direct involvement with the manufacturing sites of the company.

In the long term view, centralising the financial and administrative knowledge and operations makes financial sense resulting in improved controls and decision making efficiency. However, it is likely that SPW would have some short term financial impacts to absorb as well as working with a work force who may have low morale at work.

## Task 2.4

### Monthly operating report

| Original budget | | Flexed budget | Actual | Variance Fav/(Adv) |
|---|---|---|---|---|
| 178,000 | Sales volume (units) | | 192,000 | |
| £ | | £ | £ | £ |
| 1,281,600 | Sales revenue | 1,382,400 | 1,377,000 | –5,400 |
| | Costs | | | |
| 462,800 | Materials | 499,200 | 500,100 | –900 |
| 480,600 | Labour | 518,400 | 516,500 | 1,900 |
| 67,640 | Distribution | 72,960 | 74,200 | –1,240 |
| 60,860 | Energy | 64,640 | 65,080 | –440 |
| 24,000 | Equipment hire | 28,000 | 28,600 | –600 |
| 8,800 | Depreciation | 8,800 | 8,700 | 100 |
| 78,000 | Marketing | 78,000 | 78,900 | –900 |
| 25,600 | Administration | 25,600 | 24,820 | 780 |
| 1,208,300 | Total | 1,295,600 | 1,296,900 | –1,300 |
| | | | | |
| 73,300 | Operating profit/(loss) | 86,800 | 80,100 | –6,700 |

### Workings

Flexed sales revenue = £1,281,600 × $\dfrac{192,000}{178,000}$ = £1,382,400

Energy original budget = £12,800 fixed, so £48,060 variable

Flexed energy cost = £12,800 + $\left(£48,060 \times \dfrac{192}{178}\right)$ = £64,640

Flexed equipment hire = £24,000 × $\dfrac{7}{6}$ = £28,000

## Task 2.5

### (a) Reasons for variances

I have reviewed the results for the period. There was an operating profit of £198,000 compared with the flexed budget profit of £196,000. The original budget anticipated a profit of £227,000 based on higher sales of 165,000 units.

Compared with the original budget, the result is disappointing and this is attributed to a loss of sales volume due to price competition. The volume was 11% below the original budget despite our own 10% price reduction during the year. The flexed budget calculations indicate that lost sales should have generated a profit of £31,000 (£227,000 less £196,000). The flexed budget is based on the original but with appropriate volume adjustments.

The unforeseen competition has taken sales volume from us and forced us to make 10% price reductions. The full year impact of the price reduction is significant and we are not confident that volume will recover fully. This situation might have been avoided with better market intelligence and a proactive marketing campaign.

Compared with the flexed budget there was an adverse sales variance of £29,000 (3.8%), caused by the 10% price reduction part way through the year.

However, there was a £9,000 favourable variance on material costs (4%) where both material price and usage were lower than budgeted. Similarly, the labour cost variance was £15,000 favourable (12%). With production volumes less than budgeted there was less need to work overtime at premium rate plus better quality materials resulted in improved efficiencies and less waste requiring rework.

### (b) Setting and managing the budget

To be challenging, budgets should be stretching, always striving for improvement, whilst being achievable. We can see from the operating statement that the adverse sales variance was counterbalanced by unrelated and fortuitous favourable cost variances in materials and labour. It can be argued that the budget was poorly focused, failing to address the threat of competition and not challenging managers to improve efficiency.

I recommend that we introduce closer scrutiny at the budget setting stage to ensure that budgetary slack is not permitted and that efficiency improvements are planned and introduced. A stretching budget is likely to motivate managers to improve performance. Variances need to be fully analysed and explained on a regular basis and corrective action taken promptly.

BPP
LEARNING MEDIA

### (c)    Standard costing

Standard costing is an effective mechanism for bringing rigour to budgetary control. It makes sense to set standards for production resources at the level of a single unit of production. The standards can be multiplied by planned production levels to create cost budgets.

The system facilitates the calculation of detailed cost variances which helps managers to understand and manage the resources effectively. Looking at the operating statement, for example, we could analyse the material variance into the price and efficiency aspects and also see whether the labour variance was wholly due to saved overtime premium.

## Task 2.6

### Impact on profit of increasing fixed costs but reducing variable costs

For each unit sold, selling price minus variable costs is termed as 'contribution'; each unit sold contributes a certain amount towards covering the fixed costs of the business. When the total contribution (from all units sold) exactly matches fixed costs then the business makes a profit of zero. This is termed the break-even point. When total contribution exceeds fixed costs, the amount of the excess is profit.

If fixed costs increase, this will mean that more total contribution will need to be generated in order to cover the fixed costs. However the reduction in variable costs means that each unit generates more contribution per unit. Whether the increased contribution per unit is an advantage relative to the increased fixed costs depends on the number of units expected to be sold.

The ratio of incremental fixed costs/incremental variable cost per unit can be used to establish the number of units at which we are economically indifferent. If, for example, increased fixed costs of £10,000 are balanced by a decrease of £2 per unit, then £10,000/2 = 5,000. This tells us that if sales are likely to be below 5,000 units we would make more profit by not making the change, as the increase in fixed costs exceeds the increased contribution. If sales are likely to be above 5,000 units the increased contribution exceeds the increased fixed costs. At exactly 5,000 units the increase in fixed costs is the same as the decrease in total variable costs, and so we are indifferent.

# Task 2.7

## Limiting factors

The usual decision rule is that we should make and sell the maximum possible of the products which generate the highest amount of contribution per unit, so as to maximise total contribution and thereby profit.

When any factors of production are in short supply, we term these as 'limiting factors' in that they limit our ability to produce as much as we would like of our products which require this limited resource.

The decision rule then changes, so that we should maximise the contribution per unit of limiting factor. We calculate this by dividing contribution per unit by the quantity per unit of the limiting factor required. We should rank the three products which use this factor and produce the highest ranked product until we reach the limit of its demand. We should then do the same with the product ranked second, then third, until we have exhausted the amount of the product in short supply.

This, unlike a 20% cut across the board, focusses production on the productions which generate the most contribution per unit of limiting factor and thereby maximise profit. It should also be noted that, since only three products require this material, there is no need to reduce production across other products.

........................................................................................

# Task 2.8

## Pricing of special order

Total cost per unit includes variable cost plus the amount of fixed costs which have been absorbed into the unit, according to the business's overhead absorption method. Sales price must normally be set higher than total cost, in order to ensure that all costs, both fixed and variable, are covered.

In this particular case, the special order would be in addition to the business's normal production. Presumably the price of the normal production has been set to ensure that all costs, including the fixed costs, have been covered by the sale of the normal level of production. This means that the price on the special order only needs to be higher than the additional variable costs, as fixed costs have already been covered by normal production. Any sales price in excess of £187 will generate additional profit for the business.

At the same time, setting the price this low may not be a wise idea. If any existing customers discover that a new customer is being charged less than the normal price of £400 they are likely to be unhappy and may take their business elsewhere. If the one-off order becomes a regular order, it would be difficult for us to increase the price to a more sustainable level later.

........................................................................................

# Chapter 3 – Accounting control systems and procedures: Accounting Systems and Controls

## Task 3.1

Allocating a payment from one customer to another customer's account in order to balance the books and detract from a shortfall is called | teeming and lading | .

## Task 3.2

| | ✓ |
|---|---|
| False representation | ✓ |
| Failure to segregate duties | |
| Failure to disclose information | ✓ |
| Abuse of position | ✓ |
| Duress and undue influence | |

## Task 3.3

| Systemic weakness | Understatement of reported profit ✓ | Overstatement of reported profit ✓ |
|---|---|---|
| Overvaluation of inventory at the period end | | ✓ |
| Creating an unnecessary allowance for doubtful debts | ✓ | |
| Fictitious sales | | ✓ |
| Not writing off irrecoverable debts | | ✓ |
| Overstating expenses | ✓ | |

## Task 3.4

| Systemic weakness | Misappropriation of assets ✓ | Misstatement in the financial statements ✓ |
|---|---|---|
| Leaving offices where computers are held unlocked | ✓ | |
| Failing to maintain an asset register | | ✓ |
| Omitting inventory from the annual physical count | | ✓ |
| Creating a fictitious employee on the payroll | ✓ | ✓ |
| Failing to chase unpaid debts | | ✓ |

## Task 3.5

Segregation of duties is a type of ⎡ staff control ⎤ over fraud in the accounting system.

## Task 3.6

| No. | Weakness | Potential problem |
|---|---|---|
| 1 | The sales manager appears to have very little involvement in day to day sales, apart from negotiating terms with new customers. | Failures in the system and system abuses could go unnoticed. |
| 2 | The procedures do not include any mention of quality control checks ensuring that goods of the correct category and standard have been despatched. | If this is not happening the company could be sending out sub-standard goods. |
| 3 | Orders can be taken without agreeing a price. | The company is in a weak position to negotiate price after the goods have been despatched. |

| No. | Weakness | Potential problem |
|---|---|---|
| 4 | Despatch signs the green copy of the order, but there is no signed goods received note from the customer, confirming receipt of the goods. | Goods could be delivered to the wrong address, or no delivered at all and still charged for. This could cause problems with customer goodwill as well as creating potential for fraud. |
| 5 | Lack of authorisation of new accounts. | There should be a policy for deciding on whether to offer any credit at all. Potential for fraud through collusion with customers. |
| 6 | The terms agreed by the sales manager are not countersigned. | Potential for fraud through collusion with customers. |
| 7 | Only one signature is required on most orders. | Potential for fraud through collusion with customers. |
| 8 | The accounts receivable clerk checks, clears and arranges payment of invoices. She also handles customer queries, issues credit notes and records the receipt of payments. There is a lack of segregation of duties. | Potential for fraud through collusion with customers. |
| 9 | The sales manager and accounts receivable clerk control all aspects of sales accounting. | Potential for fraud through collusion. |
| 10 | Cash receipts are only monitored and posted once a week. | Increases the opportunity for teeming and lading, and means a bad service will be given to customers if they ring with a query. |
| 11 | No counter-signatory required for credit notes. | Potential for fraud through collusion with customers. |

## Task 3.7

| | ✓ |
|---|---|
| Physical controls | |
| Segregation of duties | ✓ |
| Management controls | |
| Supervisory controls | ✓ |
| Organisation | |
| Authorisation (approval) of transactions | ✓ |
| Arithmetic and bookkeeping checks | |
| Personnel controls | |

## Task 3.8

**Note.** Other valid weaknesses may have been identified and would gain credit.

| No. | Weakness | Potential problem |
|---|---|---|
| 1 | Only hand-written notes are made rather than a pre-numbered requisition form. | Requisition details might be lost and might not be followed up. As they are hand written, it could be difficult to read the writing and errors could be made. |
| 2 | Requisitions are not authorised. | Employees could order goods for their own use or that the business does not need. |
| 3 | Purchasing manager should obtain quotations from several suppliers. | The company could pay higher prices than necessary, hence wasting resources. |
| 4 | There is no system for recording receipt of other goods and services. | The company may pay for other goods and services which have not been received. |

| No. | Weakness | Potential problem |
|-----|----------|-------------------|
| 5 | Invoices are only matched to purchase orders 'if they are available'. There is no mention of investigating missing purchase orders. No goods should be ordered without a valid purchase order. | The company could receive goods which have not been ordered, or are not authorised. |
| 6 | Purchases ledger clerk performs too many tasks. | There is increased chance of fraud or error. |
| 7 | Invoices are not authorised before being paid. | There is increased risk of fraud or error. |

## Task 3.9

**Note.** Other valid weaknesses may have been identified and would gain credit.

| No. | Weakness | Potential problem |
|-----|----------|-------------------|
| 1 | Blank timekeeping cards are used. These should be pre-printed with the employee name and number and should be pre-numbered. | Timekeeping cards could go missing. |
| 2 | There is no supervision over the signing in or signing out and no ID is required. | Employees could record fictitious hours and employees could sign in or out for their colleagues. |
| 3 | No independent personnel function. | Supervisors and wages clerk could add fictitious employees to the payroll and misappropriate their wages. |
| 4 | Lack of segregation of duties with the wages clerk. | The wages clerk could misappropriate funds. |
| 5 | No control over weekly payroll, such as reconciling it to the prior month's payroll. | Hours worked could be incorrectly entered. |
| 6 | Only one person banks the cheque, collects the cash and draws up the pay packets. | Cash cheque could be misappropriated either before reaching wages clerk or by the wages clerk. |

| No. | Weakness | Potential problem |
|-----|----------|-------------------|
| 7 | The pay packets are not checked against the payroll and signed for by the supervisors when they take control of them. | Pay packets could be incorrect or could go missing, resulting in a loss of cash to the company (if the packets are too high) or disgruntled staff (if the packets are too low or if they are missing). |
| 8 | Employees do not count and sign for their pay packets and their IDs are not required. | Employees could claim not to have been paid, or could dispute the amount of their pay packets raising unpleasant disputes with the company, which could result in financial losses to the company. |
| 9 | Inadequate control over the distribution itself. There is only one supervisor present and it is not a formal process. | Supervisors could sign for absent or terminated employees and collect their wages. |
| 10 | No procedure for unclaimed wages. | Unclaimed wages could be misappropriated. |
| 11 | Poor control over hiring employees: job vacancies are not authorised, there is no mention of an interviewing process and no mention of authorising the employment contract. | Staff could be hired without the necessary references and qualifications. Unnecessary staff could be hired, who are not needed and fictitious staff could be created and their pay misappropriated. |
| 12 | Verbal authorisation for pay increases. | Increases could be made that are not authorised, resulting in the misappropriation of funds, or resulting in a payroll that the company cannot afford. |

# Chapter 4 – Decision making and control: Accounting Systems and Controls/Management Accounting: Decision and Control

## Task 4.1

The ❘ fixed overheads ❘ total variance may be analysed into expenditure, efficiency and capacity variances.

........................................................

## Task 4.2

**Complete the following statements:**

**(a)** The standard quantity of labour per unit is ❘ 15 ❘ minutes.

**(b)** The standard quantity of materials needed to produce 13,500 units of X07 is ❘ 16,875 ❘ litres.

**(c)** The standard labour hours to produce 12,000 units of X07 is ❘ 3,000 ❘ hours.

**(d)** The standard labour cost to produce 13,500 units of X07 is ❘ £ ❘ 57,375 ❘ .

**(e)** The standard overhead absorption rate per unit is ❘ £ 5.50 ❘

**Workings**

**(a)** 3,500 direct labour hours/14,000 units = 0.25 hours (15 minutes)

**(b)** Standard quantity per unit = 17,500 litres/14,000 units = 1.25 litres

13,500 units × 1.25 litres = 16,875 litres

**(c)** Standard labour hours per unit = 0.25 hours (see part (a))

12,000 units × 0.25 hours = 3,000 hours

**(d)** Standard labour cost per unit = £59,500/14,000 units = £4.25

13,500 units × £4.25 hours = £57,375

**(e)** Standard OAR = £77,000/14,000 units = £5.50 per unit

........................................................

## Task 4.3

### (a)

The standard cost per kilogram is | **£** | 2.50 | .

**Working**

£10,915 − £1,665 = £9,250 standard cost

Standard cost per kilogram = £9,250/3,700 kilograms = £2.50

### (b)

The material usage variance is | **£** | 6,000 | | adverse | .

**Working**

| 19,000 units should use (× 10 litres per unit) | 190,000 litres |
|---|---|
| But did use | 200,000 litres |
| Material usage variance in litres | 10,000 litres (A) |
| × standard cost per litre (£132,000/220,000 litres) | × £0.60 |
| Material usage variance in £ | £6,000 (A) |

### (c)

The total labour efficiency variance is | **£** | 4,500 | | favourable | .

The idle time variance is | **£** | 6,000 | | adverse | .

**Working**

Labour efficiency variance

| 12,000 units should have taken (× 0.6 hours) | 7,200 hrs |
|---|---|
| But did take | 6,900 hrs |
| | 300 hrs (F) |
| At standard rate | × £15.00 |
| Efficiency variance | £4,500 (F) |

Idle time variance

7,300 hours − 6,900 hours = 400 hours idle time

400 hours × £15.00 = £6,000 (A)

## Task 4.4

The fixed overhead volume variance is £ | 25,000 | favourable .

**Working**

| | £ |
|---|---|
| OAR is £350,000/28,000 = £12.50 per unit | |
| Actual production @ standard OAR 30,000 × £12.50 | 375,000 |
| Budgeted production @ standard OAR 28,000 × £12.50 | 350,000 |
| Volume variance | 25,000 (F) |

The actual fixed production overheads incurred were £ | 315,000 .

**Working**

| | £ |
|---|---|
| Budgeted overhead | 350,000 |
| Actual overhead (Balancing figure) | 315,000 |
| Expenditure variance | 35,000 (F) |

## Task 4.5

| Variance | Amount £ | Adverse/ Favourable |
|---|---|---|
| Fixed overhead capacity | 448,000 | favourable |
| Fixed overhead efficiency | 268,000 | adverse |

**Workings**

Fixed overhead capacity variance

| | £ |
|---|---|
| OAR is £3,840,000/480,000 = £8.00 per labour hour | |
| Actual hours @ standard OAR 536,000 × £8.00 | 4,288,000 |
| Budgeted hours @ standard OAR 480,000 × £8.00 | 3,840,000 |
| Capacity variance | 448,000 (F) |

Fixed overhead efficiency variance

| | £ |
|---|---|
| Standard hours for actual production @ standard OAR 67,000 × 7.5 hours × £8.00 | 4,020,000 |
| Actual hours @ standard OAR 536,000 × £8.00 | 4,288,000 |
| Efficiency variance | 268,000 (A) |

## Task 4.6

| | | | £ |
|---|---|---|---|
| Budgeted variable cost for actual production | | | 387,600 |
| Budgeted fixed cost | | | 234,000 |
| Total budgeted cost for actual production | | | 621,600 |

| Variance | Favourable £ | Adverse £ | |
|---|---|---|---|
| Direct materials price | 18,700 | | |
| Direct materials usage | 11,900 | | |
| Direct labour rate | | 28,560 | |
| Direct labour efficiency | | 12,240 | |
| Fixed overhead expenditure | 13,000 | | |
| Fixed overhead volume | N/A | N/A | |
| Total variance | 43,600 | 40,800 | –2,800 |
| Actual cost of actual production | | | 618,800 |

### Workings

Budgeted variable cost per unit = (£130,200 + £223,200)/12,400 units = £28.50

Budgeted variable cost for actual production = 13,600 units × £28.50 = £387,600

Total budgeted cost for actual production = £387,600 + £234,000 (fixed costs)

= £621,600

Direct labour efficiency variance

| 13,600 units should have taken (× 2 hours) | 27,200 hrs |
|---|---|
| But did take | 28,560 hrs |
| | 1,360 hrs (A) |
| At standard rate | × £9.00 |
| Efficiency variance | £12,240 (A) |

Fixed overhead expenditure variance = Actual £13,000 lower than budgeted, so favourable.

●●●●●●●●●●●●●●●●●●●●●●●●●●●●●●●●●●●●●●●●●●●●●●●●●●●●●●●●●●●●●●●●●●●●●●●●●●●●●●●●●

## Task 4.7

### (a)

The part of the variance explained by the increase in the price index is

£ | 281,250 (A)  .

**Working**

| | £ |
|---|---|
| 12,500 litres × £450 (original standard rate) | 5,625,000 |
| 12,500 litres × £472.50 (£450 × 126.525/120.50) | 5,906,250 |
| | 281,250 (A) |

### (b)

The part of the variance not explained by the increase in the price index is

£ | 93,750  .

**Working**

£375,000 – £281,250 = £93,750

**(c)**

The percentage increase in the index is [ 5 ] %.

**Working**

(126.525 – 120.50)/120.50 = 0.05 (5%)

**(d)**

|  | September 20X3 £ | December 20X3 £ |
|---|---|---|
| Cost per kilogram of Z4QX | 2,136.62 | 2,543.84 |

**Workings**

Difference between April 20X3 and May 20X3 = £135.74

Difference between May 20X3 and June 20X3 = £135.74

September 20X3 cost = £1,729.40 (June 20X3) + (£135.74 × 3) = £2,136.62

December 20X3 cost = £2,136.62 (September X3) + (£135.74 × 3) = £2,543.84

**(e)**

The forecast cost per kilogram, using the regression line, for September 20X3 is £ [ 118.85 ] .

**Workings**

June 20X3 is period 41. Therefore September 20X3 = period 44.

y = 24.69 + 2.14x        where y = cost per kilogram        x = the period

y = 24.69 + (2.14 × 44)

y = £118.85

## Task 4.8

### Total direct material variance

The total direct material variance simply compares the **flexed budget** for materials with the actual cost incurred. The flexed budget is the total budgeted cost of materials for the actual production; 21,000 units in this example. It is incorrect to calculate the variance as £74,500 adverse by comparing the actual cost of £954,500 with the original budgeted cost of £880,000.

The flexing of the budget calculates the **quantity of materials** which are expected to be used to produce the **actual production**. Therefore, the expected usage of materials to produce 21,000 units is £924,000 (if 80,000 kilograms costing £880,000 is required to make 20,000 units then it follows, assuming that the material cost and quantity is perfectly variable, that to make 21,000 units requires 84,000 kilograms at a cost of £11 per kilogram (£880,000/80,000)).

This flexed budget can now be **compared with the actual** costs to produce the total material variance of £30,500. This variance is adverse because the **actual cost was greater than the flexed budgeted cost**.

This total variance can now be split into two elements:

- The variance due to the price being different to that which was expected: the material price variance.

- The variance due to the quantity of material used per unit of production being different to that which was expected: the material usage variance.

The expected (standard or budgeted or planned) price is £11 per kilogram (£880,000/80,000) and therefore the expected cost of 83,000 kilograms must be 83,000 kilograms at £11 per kilogram. This is £913,000.

The price variance can now be calculated by taking the actual cost (price paid) for the 83,000 kilograms and comparing this to the expected cost. This results in £913,000, compared to £954,500: a variance of £41,500. This variance is adverse because the **actual cost is greater than the expected cost**.

The material usage variance is calculated by taking the quantity of materials which would be expected to be used to produce the actual volume of production. In this case 21,000 units were produced and the expected quantity of materials for each unit is 4 kilograms (80,000 kilograms/20,000 units). Therefore, to produce 21,000 units requires 84,000 kilograms of material. Compare this to the actual quantity used of 83,000 kilograms produces a variance of 1,000 kilograms. This is favourable and needs to be **valued at the expected cost** of £11 per kilogram, giving £11,000.

The usage variance is always **valued at the standard cost** (expected/planned or budgeted) because the price variance has already been isolated. If both variances have been calculated correctly they should reconcile back to the total materials variance. In this example, the price variance of £41,500 adverse less the £11,000 favourable usage variance is reconciled to the total variance of £30,500 adverse.

# Task 4.9

## (a)

|  | Scenario 1 | Scenario 2 |
|---|---|---|
| Return on capital employed | 11.96% | 9.52% |
| Inventory holding period in days | 50.00 | 45.29 |
| Sales price per unit | £14.00 | £12.00 |
| Full production cost per unit | £9.00 | £9.00 |

### Workings

Return on capital employed
Scenario 1 = £275,000/£2,298,400 × 100% = 11.96%
Scenario 2 = £200,000/£2,100,340 × 100% = 9.52%

Inventory holding period
Scenario 1 = £147,950/(£1,680,000 – £600,000) × 365 = 50.00 days
Scenario 2 = £167,500/(£1,800,000 – £450,000) × 365 = 45.29 days

Sales price per unit
Scenario 1 = £1,680,000/120,000 = £14.00
Scenario 2 = £1,800,000/150,000 = £12.00

Full production cost per unit
Scenario 1 = (£1,680,000 – £600,000)/120,000 = £9.00
Scenario 2 = (£1,800,000 – £450,000)/150,000 = £9.00

## (b)

|  | Scenario 3 |
|---|---|
| Capital employed (£) | 175,000 |
| Return on capital employed (%) | 13 |
| Profit margin (%) | 14 |
| Gearing (%) | 32.75 |
| Profit (to the nearest £) | 22,750 |
| Sales revenue (to the nearest £) | 162,500 |

### Workings

Profit (to the nearest £) = £175,000 × (13/100) = £22,750

Sales revenue (to the nearest £) = £22,750 ÷ (14/100) = £162,500

**(c)**

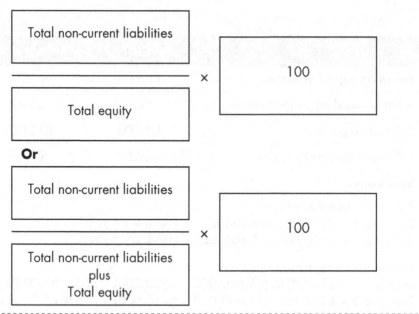

$$\frac{\text{Total non-current liabilities}}{\text{Total equity}} \times 100$$

**Or**

$$\frac{\text{Total non-current liabilities}}{\begin{array}{c}\text{Total non-current liabilities}\\ \text{plus}\\ \text{Total equity}\end{array}} \times 100$$

## Task 4.10

**(a)**

|  | Product Tig £ | Product Tag £ |
|---|---|---|
| The contribution per unit is | 1,200 | 1,350 |
| The contribution per kilogram of materials is | 200 | 180 |

**Workings**

Contribution per unit

Product Tig = £4,000 – £2,800 = £1,200
Product Tag = £4,950 – £3,600 = £1,350

Contribution per kilogram of material

Product Tig = £1,200/6 kg = £200
Product Tag = £1,350/7.5 kg = £180

**(b)**

The optimal production order for products Tig and Tag is Tig then Tag .

(Based on the contribution per kilogram of material calculated in part (a)).

**(c)**

|  | Product Tig | Product Tag |
|---|---|---|
| Production in units | 200 | 240 |

**Workings**

Supply is limited to 3,000 kilograms of material

Product Tig then Tag (based on part (b))

200 units of Tig × 6 kg per unit = 1,200 kg (so 1,800 kg remaining to produce Tag)

1,800 kg/7.5 kg per unit = 240 units of Tag

**(d)**

|  | Product Tig £ | Product Tag £ |
|---|---|---|
| Total contribution | 240,000 | 324,000 |

**Workings**

Product Tig = 200 units × £1,200 = £240,000
Product Tag = 240 units × £1,350 = £324,000

**(e)**

| Should Alpha Ltd purchase the additional material? | Give a reason |
|---|---|
| **(1)** Yes | **(2)** The additional cost per kilogram is less than the contribution per kilogram. |

## Task 4.11

**(a)**

|  | Sales price £40 | Sales price £50 |
|---|---|---|
| The target total production cost per unit | £28 | £35 |
| The target fixed production cost per unit | £16 | £22 |
| The target total fixed production cost | £8,000,000 | £9,460,000 |

### Workings

Target total production cost per unit
Sales price £40 = £40 × 70/100 = £28
Sales price £50 = £50 × 70/100 = £35

Target fixed production cost per unit
Sales price £40 = £28 – £12 = £16
Sales price £50 = £35 – £13 = £22

Target fixed production cost
Sales price £40 = £16 per unit × 500,000 = £8,000,000
Sales price £50 = £22 per unit × 430,000 = £9,460,000

**(b)**

Alpha should set the price at  | £50 |  in order to achieve the target profit margin.

........................................................................................

## Task 4.12

**To:** Finance director       **Subject:** Variances
**From:** Accounting technician    **Date:** Today

**(a) Sales volume**

The sales volume is expected to double.

The volume increase will increase the profit margin if the fixed costs remain constant.

In this case the fixed production costs are remaining unchanged and therefore the increased volume will improve the gross profit margin (GPM).

**Materials cost**

The material cost per unit reduces by 20% to £4 per unit which will also improve the margin for the proposed position. The doubling of the volume is likely to allow the company to purchase in greater quantities and access additional discounts.

**Labour cost**

The labour cost per unit is unchanged and therefore has no effect on the margin.

There have been no economies of scale or learning effect.

### Fixed production costs

The fixed production costs are constant in total but the important point is that they are spread over more units. The proposed position increases the volume by 2x (200%) which reduces the fixed cost per unit. Fixed costs per unit reduce by 50%. This will improve the margin for the proposed position.

## (b) Inventory levels

Inventory levels are likely to increase significantly because the volume of demand is expected to be higher and therefore higher inventory levels will be needed to fulfil orders. Based upon the current inventory levels in relation to turnover the forecast position will be that inventory levels may increase to around £560,000 (current inventory days = 350,000/ 2,250,000 × 365 = 56.78 days, therefore inventory will become (£3.6 million/365) × 56.78 days = £560,000).

### Trade receivable levels

Trade receivables' levels are likely to increase significantly because the turnover increases. The current position is that trade receivable days are 55.3 days (500/3,300) × 365. Therefore assuming similar profile trade receivables will increase to around £820k (5,400,000/365) × 55.3 = £818k.

# Task 4.13

## (a) Credit controller

Currently the assessment of creditworthiness, setting of credit limits, and chasing of debts is performed by sales staff. Sales staff may not have experience in credit control and may, while acting entirely with good intentions, extend credit to a customer who is not credit worthy. They could be tempted to give credit to customers without thoroughly checking their financial situation. Sales staff should not be responsible for chasing overdue receivables, as they may be reluctant to push hard for payment for fear of damaging the relationship with customers. They are also likely to see the task as low priority and prefer to spend their time generating sales and thereby gaining commission.

The new credit controller should perform a thorough assessment of new customers before setting a credit limit, which should be authorised by the sales manager. The credit controller should chase payment of overdue receivables, which should happen before they are 120 days overdue.

### Sales manager

Sales staff have freedom to set sales discounts, and may set unrealistic discounts to achieve their sales targets. SSSL then loses out on potential revenue. Sales staff are also able to access the customer master file to enter discounts, which could result in fraud or error.

The sales manager should set out clear policies for the award of discounts and then authorise any discounts given. The sales manager should then update the master files. The sales manager should also introduce procedures to improve the documentation in the sales system, such as having sequentially numbered sales orders rather than an email to the accounting and despatch departments. As stated above, the sales manager should also authorise credit limits.

### (b) Cost implications

SSSL will have additional payroll costs to bear. The credit controller's salary will be a fixed cost but the sales manager's salary is likely to be semi-variable, as the role is likely to carry some sales-related remuneration. These costs will increase the break-even point and impact on profit, although hopefully the involvement of the sales manager will increase sales and that of the credit controller will reduce bad debt expenses.

### Resentment of sales staff

The filling of these two roles could cause resentment among sales staff. They will lose a lot of their freedom to operate autonomously , may interpret the appointments as being criticism of their abilities, and could be obstructive. They could leave SSSL, leaving the company with a shortage of experienced staff.

........................................................................................

## Task 4.14

If Roe were to stop being produced, the company would lose the benefit of the contribution generated by Roe, but would save on the fixed costs:

|  | £ |
|---|---|
| Loss of contribution | (30,000) |
| Savings in fixed costs | 10,000 |
| Incremental loss | (20,000) |

If production stopped on Roe, the company would see a fall of £20,000 in their profits.

The profit generated by Codlings would be as follows:

|  | £ |
|---|---|
| Contribution | 24,000 |
| Directly attributable fixed costs | (12,000) |
| Incremental profit | 12,000 |

If production was switched to Codlings, Gritby would only make £12,000 profit, so the company would suffer an overall drop in profits of £8,000.

They should, therefore, keep making Roe in preference to Codlings.

## Task 4.15

**(a)**

|  | Blossom £000 | |
|---|---|---|
| Revenue (2,850 × 1.4) | 3,990.0 | |
| Materials (784 × 1.4 × 0.95) | 1,042.7 | |
| Direct labour (448 × 1.4) | 627.2 | |
| Fixed production overheads (420 + 100) | 520.0 | |
| Cost of sales | 2,189.9 | |
| Gross profit | 1,800.1 | 45.1% |
| Sales and distribution costs (640 × 1.4) | 896.0 | |
| Administration costs (250 + 60) | 310.0 | |
| Profit from operations | 594.1 | 14.9% |

**(b)**

Dandelion should be closed down if the decision was based solely on the financial data.

(1) This is because the company will be more profitable:
(2) Current profit = £150,000 + £308,000 = £458,000
(3) New profit = £594,100

**(c)** **Any one of the following suggested answers.**

- **Staff morale** – staff will either need to be redeployed or made redundant, which negatively impacts morale and motivation.

- **Customers** – as the product made and sold by Dandelion is different from that of Blossom and the local retailers do not buy from both subsidiaries, it is possible that Daisy could adversely impact the success of these local retailers. The Dandelion range sources from local materials, which is unique selling point. By ceasing this range, Daisy could adversely impact their company image, and potentially even impact the Blossom range's appeal.

- **Suppliers** – some suppliers may be reliant on the organisation to stay in business. If the organisation chooses to stop making the product this could have severe consequences on these local suppliers, especially the local wood supplier.

## Task 4.16

**(a)**

The loss of a proportion of financial and customer staff will likely have affected staff morale amongst the remaining staff in these departments. This could have affected their commitment to the company and been detrimental to the customer experience. Less staff could also have affected accuracy and there could potentially be errors in the accounts.

- The reduction in staff is likely to explain some of the reduction of £774,000 in administrative expenses (financial staff) and increase in distribution costs (of £1,010,000) due to the increase in warehouse staff.

- By moving the focus of the business to increasing sales, these sales may be made at all costs, with large discounts (affecting the gross profit) and/or risking higher bad debt levels. Controls need to be in place to ensure that sales staff are following company policies regarding discounting and offering credit.

- Flexing the budget will give a more useful figure for costs and revenues to compare with the actual costs and revenues generated. These variances will help to identify where sales are being made at the expense of profits caused by heavy discounting by sales staff.

- The company's profit has decreased, yet the corporation tax charge has risen. This may suggest issues regarding the computation of the tax during the year. There may be a lack of knowledge remaining in the financial department to complete the tax return correctly, and taking advantage of any reliefs.

**(b)**

- The company has increased its revenues by 12% and its gross profit by 16% which in a competitive market is very good. However, increased operating expenses have resulted in a reduction in operating profits of 20%.

- The gross margin is very high; this is not abnormal in this sector, especially for software (although the margin is high for hardware), but it may also be the result of errors, due to the staff turnover.

- Total expenses as a percentage of revenue have increased substantially in 20X3 (47%) compared with expenses in 20X2 (30%). The result of this has seen operating profit as a percentage of revenue reducing significantly year on year from 48% (20X2) to 34% (20X3).

- The increase in the distribution costs as a percentage of revenue (an increase of 5%) may reflect inefficiencies in the method of distribution in an industry that separates these functions.

- The administrative expenses as a percentage of revenue have halved from 13% to 7%, although they do not represent a significant amount in absolute terms. This is possibly due to the reduction in financial and administrative staff during the year.

- The increase in the selling expenses as a percentage of revenue by 18% may be as a result of the need for the company to spend more on advertising and the hiring of new sales staff.

- The reduction in profit before tax and the increased tax charge have resulted in a reduction in profit after tax of 43%.

- Total dividends have increased, despite the lower profits. This may be due to pressure from shareholders or a lack of investment in the business (by reinvesting profits made) as a Board of Directors decision.

# Chapter 5 – Ratio analysis: Accounting Systems and Controls/Financial Statements of Limited Companies/Management Accounting: Decision and Control

## Task 5.1

|  | ✓ |
|---|---|
| Receivables days + Inventory days – Payables days | ✓ |
| Receivables days + Payables days – Inventory days | |
| Inventory days + Receivables days + Payables days | |
| Inventory days – Receivables days – Payables days | |

## Task 5.2

### (a)

|  | ✓ |
|---|---|
| Understandability | |
| Relevance | ✓ |
| Comparability | |
| Faithful representation | ✓ |

### (b)

Income is defined as:

'Increases in economic benefits during the accounting period in the form of inflows or enhancements of assets or decreases of liabilities that result in increases in equity, other than those relating to contributions from equity participants'.

# Task 5.3

## (a)

| Return on equity | Profit after tax/Total equity × 100 |
|---|---|
| Acid test ratio | (Current assets – Inventories)/Current liabilities |
| Inventory holding period | Inventories/Cost of sales × 365 |
| Asset turnover (net assets) | Revenue/(Total assets – Current liabilities) |
| Gearing | Non-current liabilities/(Total equity + Non-current liabilities) × 100 |

## (b) Ratios:

| Ratio | Calculation | Working |
|---|---|---|
| Return on equity | **18.1%** | 5,136/28,326 |
| Acid test ratio | **0.9:1** | (13,192 – 6,724)/7,258 |
| Inventory holding period | **58.3 days** | 6,724/42,126 × 365 |
| Asset turnover (net assets) | **1.2 times** | 58,914/(55,984 – 7,258) |
| Gearing | **41.9%** | 20,400/(28,326 + 20,400) |

# Task 5.4

## (a)

**Current ratio**

- Current ratio is better than the industry average

- Poole Ltd has more current assets available to meet its current liabilities/is more solvent

- However, the ratio looks to be too high and indicates less efficient management of working capital

- It may have higher levels of receivables, inventories or cash and cash equivalents/lower payables

### Inventory turnover

- Inventory turnover is better than the industry average

- Poole Ltd is selling its inventories slightly more quickly as compared to the industry average

- Could be due to more effective inventory management systems or the company might have reduced its selling prices or employed better marketing techniques

- Leads to lower storage costs and there is less risk of stock obsolescence

### Trade receivables collection period

- Trade receivables collection period is worse than the industry average

- Poole Ltd is taking longer to collect debts

- This is bad for cash flow

- Could be due to poor credit control procedures

- May just be offering longer credit terms to boost sales

- Could indicate the presence of irrecoverable debts

### Trade payables payment period

- Trade payables payment period may be considered to be better than the industry average (if linked to supplier goodwill) or worse (if linked to cash flow)

- Poole Ltd is paying its trade suppliers sooner

- This is bad for cash flow

- This is good for supplier goodwill

- It may have negotiated additional settlement discounts with suppliers

- Suppliers may have dictated shorter payment terms

**(b)**

Collect debts more quickly/reduce trade receivable days, eg improve debt collection procedures, reduce credit periods

Problem: possible loss of customers

Increase the length of time taken to pay suppliers/increase trade payable days, eg negotiate extended credit terms, improve payment procedures

Problem: may lose supplier goodwill/settlement discounts

Increase the inventory turnover by reducing the inventory holding

Problem: run the risk of a stock-out, which in turn, may reduce customer goodwill

## Task 5.5

### (a)

| | ✓ |
|---|---|
| Financial perspectives of the company, such as profit margins | ✓ · |
| Supplier perspectives, such as the number of supplier complaints | |
| Customer perspectives of the company, such as number of repeat orders | ✓ |

The four perspectives of the Balanced Scorecard are: customer, financial, innovation and learning, and internal perspectives.

### (b)

| Abbas Ltd Balanced Scorecard | Year ended 31 Dec 20X4 | Year ended 31 Dec 20X5 | Working |
|---|---|---|---|
| **Profitability and gearing:** | | | |
| Gross profit % | 54.3% | 50.5% | 8,640/17,120 × 100 |
| Operating profit % | 12.5% | 12.6% | 2,150/17,120 × 100 |
| Return on capital employed | 23.9% | 26.0% | 2,150/(7,190 + 1,070) × 100 |
| Gearing | 30.1% | 13.0% | 1070/(7190 + 1070) × 100 |
| **Liquidity ratios:** | | | |
| Current ratio | 2.9:1 | 2.6:1 | (10,310 – 5,060)/(1,670 + 380) |
| Acid test/quick ratio | 1.3:1 | 1.1:1 | (2,010 + 340)/(1,670 + 380) |

| Abbas Ltd Balanced Scorecard | Year ended 31 Dec 20X4 | Year ended 31 Dec 20X5 | Working |
|---|---|---|---|
| **Working capital days:** | | | |
| Inventory holding period | 119 days | 125 days | 2,900/8,480 × 365 |
| Trade receivables collection period | 41 days | 43 days | 2,010/17,120 × 365 |
| Trade payables payment period | 55 days | 72 days | 1,670/8,480 × 365 |
| Working capital cycle | 105 days | 96 days | 125 + 43 – 72 |

(c)  (i)  **Profitability**

| | ✓ |
|---|---|
| This has been a year of steady, if unspectacular, progress. Although profitability has dipped, the return on capital employed has been kept under control. | |
| The profitability ratios give cause for concern. The small increase in sales revenue has not improved the gross profit percentage. Operating expenses have increased, reducing operating profit and return on capital employed. | |
| The ratios give mixed messages. Some have improved and some have deteriorated. Further investigation is required. | ✓ |

(ii)  **Gearing**

| | ✓ |
|---|---|
| The decreased gearing ratio is due to the repayment of non-current liabilities. | ✓ |
| It is likely that the interest cover ratio has decreased. | |
| The increased gearing ratio shows that the company has become more risky. | |

### (iii) Liquidity

| | ✓ |
|---|---|
| Both ratios have deteriorated which indicates that the company is less solvent than last year, however both ratios still fall within an acceptable level. | ✓ |
| Both ratios remain quite high, which may indicate that working capital is not being used effectively. | |
| Some liquidity ratios have improved and some have deteriorated. Further investigation is required to understand whether liquidity is improving. | |

### (iv) Working capital

| | ✓ |
|---|---|
| The working capital cycle has worsened. The inventory holding period has improved but the other ratios indicate a lack of financial control. | |
| There is a welcome improvement in the working capital cycle, mainly due to the change in the payment period for payables. | ✓ |
| The working capital cycle is worse than a year ago because of the increased revenue. | |

### (v) Overall performance

| | ✓ |
|---|---|
| Profitability has declined in 20X5. However, the gearing and liquidity measures show an improving financial position. | |
| 20X5 has been a bad year. Profitability has declined and finances are coming under pressure. | |
| Steady progress has been made in 20X5. The ratios show that the company is being better managed. | ✓ |

## Task 5.6

### Increase in the current ratio

This may indicate increased inventory, cash or receivable levels. The implications of this may be that the company is expanding, or alternatively that it is experiencing trading difficulties and is unable to sell its inventory or to collect its receivables. An increase may also be due to a decrease in trade payables or other current liabilities.

### Decrease in gross profit margin

This may indicate that the cost of raw materials or bought-in goods has increased, or that discounts or selling prices have decreased. This may not be a bad thing if the reason for this is an overall increase in turnover.

### Increase in inventory holding period

An increase in inventory holding period may indicate that the company is unable to sell its inventory. An increase can also indicate that the company is expecting additional sales, or simply that the business is expanding. Many businesses are cyclical and increases and decreases are to be expected.

### An increase in gearing

Gearing is the relationship between equity and borrowings. A high level of gearing generally indicates that the company has a high level of borrowings and must pay fixed interest on the borrowings. This means that there is less available for shareholders but it may also mean that the company is expanding, which means greater returns for shareholders in the future. A high gearing ratio may mean that the company is at risk of financial problems.

••••••••••••••••••••••••••••••••••••••••••••••••••••••••••••••••••••••••••••

## Task 5.7

### (a)

|  | ✓ |
|---|---|
| An architectural practice |  |
| A supermarket |  |
| An estate agent |  |
| A manufacturer | ✓ |

The high inventory turnover rules out the estate agency and architectural practice. Supermarkets can also have a high inventory turnover, but tend to operate on low profit margin.

**(b)**

|  | ✓ |
|---|---|
| 5.1% | ✓ |
| 4.7% |  |
| 6.6% |  |
| 6% |  |

|  | **£000** |
|---|---|
| Profit before interest and tax | 230 % |
| Capital employed (3,500 + 1,000) | 4,500 |
|  | = 5.1% |

**(c)**

|  | ✓ |
|---|---|
| Reducing the receivables collection period |  |
| Reducing the inventory holding period |  |
| Reducing the payables payment period | ✓ |
| Reducing time taken to produce goods |  |

This will reduce working capital and means that it will take longer to build up working capital needed for production. The other options will all speed up the operating cycle.

**(d)**

|  | ✓ |
|---|---|
| 3.9% | ✓ |
| 7.6% |  |
| 16.1% |  |
| 7.1% |  |

Operating profit margin is a component of ROCE, so 16.3%/4.19 = 3.9%

## Task 5.8

### (a)

| | Peas | Carrots |
|---|---|---|
| ROCE | $= \dfrac{(1,500 - 240) \times 100}{(5,500 + 3,000)}$ $= 14.8\%$ | $= \dfrac{(2,500 - 500) \times 100}{(2,800 + 6,200)}$ $= 22.2\%$ |
| Gross profit margin | $= 1,500/12,000 \times 100$ $= 12.5\%$ | $= 2,500/20,500 \times 100$ $= 12.2\%$ |
| Operating profit margin | $= \dfrac{(1,500 - 240) \times 100}{12,000}$ $= 10.5\%$ | $= \dfrac{(2,500 - 500) \times 100}{20,500}$ $= 9.8\%$ |
| Current ratio | $= 5,000/4,100$ $= 1.2{:}1$ | $= 7,300/5,700$ $= 1.3{:}1$ |
| Closing inventory holding period | $= \dfrac{2,000}{10,500} \times 365$ $= 70$ days | $= \dfrac{3,600}{18,000} \times 365$ $= 73$ days |
| Trade receivables collection period | $= \dfrac{2,400}{12,000} \times 365$ $= 73$ days | $= \dfrac{3,700}{20,500} \times 365$ $= 66$ days |
| Trade payables payment period | $= \dfrac{3,100}{10,500} \times 365$ $= 108$ days | $= \dfrac{3,800}{18,000} \times 365$ $= 77$ days |
| Gearing | $= \dfrac{3,000 \times 100}{(3,000 + 5,500)}$ $= 35.3\%$ | $= \dfrac{6,200 \times 100}{(6,200 + 2,800)}$ $= 68.9\%$ |
| Interest cover | $= \dfrac{(1,050 + 210)}{210}$ $= 6$ times | $= \dfrac{(1,400 + 600)}{600}$ $= 3.3$ times |
| Dividend cover | $= 900/250$ $= 3.6$ times | $= 1,000/700$ $= 1.4$ times |

**(b) Profitability**

Carrots has an ROCE 50% higher than Peas, which is driven by the higher sales and operating profits values. Carrots' operating profit is 60% higher than Peas' operating profit. They both have a similar capital employed. This means that Carrots is more efficient at using its resources to generate income.

The gross profit margins and operating profit margins are very similar, meaning that they are equally good at controlling their costs.

**Gearing**

Carrots has approximately double the gearing of Peas, due to its higher borrowings. Carrots' interest cover is 3.3 times compared to six times for Peas, making its level of risk higher.

In a bad year Carrots could have trouble servicing its debts and have nothing left to pay to shareholders.

However, the fact that Carrots has chosen to operate with a higher level of gearing rather than raise funds from a share issue also increases the potential return to shareholders.

**Liquidity**

Peas and Carrots have broadly similar current ratios, but showing a slightly higher level of risk in the case of Carrots. Carrots is also running an overdraft while Peas has a positive cash balance.

Peas is pursuing its receivables slightly less aggressively than Carrots, but taking significantly longer to pay its suppliers.

As this does not appear to be due to shortage of cash, it must be due to Peas being able to negotiate more favourable terms than Carrots.

**Summary**

Carrots has a higher revenue than Peas and a policy of paying out most of its earnings to shareholders. This makes it an attractive proposition from a shareholder viewpoint.

However, if its revenue were to fall, there would be little left to distribute. This is the risk and return of a highly geared company.

Carrots is already running an overdraft and so has no cash to invest in any more plant and equipment. In the light of this, its dividend policy is not particularly wise. Peas has a lower revenue and a much more conservative dividend policy but may be a better long-term investment.

Forrest's decision will probably depend upon its attitude to risk and the relative purchase prices of Peas and Carrots.

# Task 5.9

## (a)

|  | 20X1 | 20X0 |
|---|---|---|
| Net profit % | = 3,000/25,500 × 100<br>= 11.8% | = 2,500/17,250 × 100<br>= 14.5% |
| Operating profit % | = 5,900/25,500 × 100<br>= 23.1% | = 3,600/17,250 × 100<br>= 20.9% |
| Gross profit % | = 10,700/25,500 × 100<br>= 42% | = 6,900/17,250 × 100<br>= 40% |
| ROCE | = 5,900/18,500 × 100<br>= 31.9% | = 3,600/9,250 × 100<br>= 38.9% |
| ROE | = 3,000/9,500<br>= 31.6% | = 2,500/7,250<br>= 34.5% |
| Gearing | = 9,000/(9,000 + 9,500)<br>    × 100<br>= 48.7% | = 2,000/(2,000 + 7,250)<br>    × 100<br>= 21.6% |
| Interest cover | = 5,900/650<br>= 9.1 times | = 3,600/100<br>= 36 times |
| Current ratio | = 6,000/5,200<br>= 1.2:1 | = 7,200/3,350<br>= 2.2: 1 |
| Quick ratio | = (6,000 – 3,600)/5,200<br>= 0.5:1 | = (7,200 – 1,800)/3,350<br>= 1.6:1 |

---

(b) **Profitability**

Revenue has increased by 48% while profit for the year has only increased by 20%. However, on closer inspection, we can see that this is to a large degree attributable to the tax charge for the year. The pre-tax profit has increased by 50%, which is in line with the increased revenue.

We do not have a breakdown of the tax charge but it could include underpayments in previous years, which distorts the trading results.

The gross profit margin and operating profit margin are very similar to the prior year, both showing a slight improvement.

There has been a significant increase in capital employed during the year ended 31.12. 20X1. There is an additional £12.3 million in non-current assets, financed from a new issue of 8% loan notes. This has had the effect of reducing the return on capital employed slightly, but not nearly as much as would be expected, indicating that the investment is already producing returns.

The return on equity is skewed by the tax charge, without which, it would be showing a slight increase due to the increased profits.

**Gearing**

The increase in loan capital does have significance for shareholders. The interest charge has increased from £100,000 to £650,000, which reduces the amount available for dividends.

Gearing has increased significantly. The rate that TTP has to offer to loan note holders has already increased from 5% to 8%. If it required further borrowing, with this high gearing, it would have to pay substantially more.

Shares in TTP have become a riskier investment. One indicator of this is the interest cover, which has fallen from 36 times to 9 times.

**Liquidity**

The area in which there is most cause for concern is liquidity. Cash has fallen by £4.2 million and the company is now running an overdraft.

It has tax to pay of £2.2 million and this will incur penalties if it is not paid on time. The current ratio has declined from 2.1:1 to 1.2:1 and the quick ratio, which indicates the immediate cash situation, shows a fall from 1.6:1 to 0.5:1, which is a dangerous position to be in.

## Summary

Overall, shareholders should be reassured that TTP is profitable and expanding. The company has perhaps overstretched itself and significantly raised its gearing, but it is to be hoped that the investment for which this cash was presumably used will bring in future returns, which should help with the liquidity issues, as long as the company manages to stay solvent until then.

# Chapter 6 – Internal controls: Accounting Systems and Controls/Financial Statements of Limited Companies/Management Accounting: Budgeting/Management Accounting: Decision and Control

## Task 6.1

Rees Ltd's plan is [ an incremental ] change.

The fact that the time of Rees Ltd's accounting staff will be freed up by not having to complete cheques by hand is [ a tangible benefit of the change ].

## Task 6.2

**(a)**

A key strength is that no customer order for even a single high value item is accepted without authorisation by the sales manager, and higher value orders must also be approved by the sales director. This reduces the exposure of the company to incurring the cost of making bespoke furniture to customer order and then finding that it is not actually a valid sale.

**(b)**

There does not appear to be a firm price agreed with the customer for the furniture ordered. It may be that the uncertainty surrounds discounts or the firm price is agreed once production have priced each job. If this is the case then the procedures need to be explicit on this point. If in fact there is no firm price agreed then the business is exposed to the risk that the customer, on receipt of the goods, refuses to pay or only pays a smaller sum than the company is due.

**(c)**

As well as a firm price being agreed with the customer at the time the order is taken, and this being approved by the sales manager and sales director where relevant, the company should get the customer to pay a deposit to the company. This will give it more assurance that the furniture will be accepted and fully paid for once delivered. It will also improve the company's working capital cycle.

## Task 6.3

**(a)**

The procedures include a robust process for ensuring that orders are taken only from new customers who represent a good credit risk. It is also a strength that, depending on the outcome of the checks, the sales manager has the discretion to require payment in full upfront or payment on credit terms. The business benefits from these in that there should be no irrecoverable debts, and cash flow should be maintained.

**(b)**

It is possibly a weakness that credit checks etc are only performed on new customers. Existing customers should also be reviewed, depending on their history with the company and the length of time since they last bought. As it is the company may still be exposed to poor payment.

It is a serious weakness that the accounts receivable clerk creates and posts invoices, has sole discretion to issue credit notes, and identifies and posts receipts. This lack of segregation of duties creates a serious risk of fraud by the clerk, alone or in collusion with a customer. The sales manager should authorise invoices and credit notes, and someone else should be responsible for identifying receipts and posting them.

**(c)**

It seems strange that a credit customer is offered 15% discount for early payment, when no such discount is offered to customers who must pay in advance. It is possible that orders are being lost through this policy, or alternatively that revenue for an agreed sale is being lost unnecessarily. The company could consider offering a discount to cash customers, and a reduced discount to early-paying credit customers.

## Task 6.4

**(a)**

**(i)** The highest value items – for production and for capital expenditure – require senior management authority before being ordered, and all purchases except the most minor require proper purchase orders. Staff understand therefore that proper procedures must be followed before items can be purchased, which reduces the risk of unnecessary items being bought by the company or that staff will purchase items for themselves at the company's expense.

**(ii)** A coherent approach is taken towards negotiating credit terms with suppliers, which benefits the company's cash flow and planning.

**(b)**

    **(i)** It appears items can be purchased from suppliers without a price having been agreed upon. This introduces unnecessary uncertainty into the company's costs and cash flows, and may mean that some items that should be authorised are bought without authority. The remedy is that no purchase orders may be raised without an agreed price being stated on them.

    **(ii)** There is no security over the purchase order forms, so in theory any staff member or other person may obtain a form and purchase items to the account of Sleeptight Ltd. This means the company may be liable to pay for items it has not received or does not want. Purchases should not be allowed to proceed unless a purchase order number, taken from the purchase order book which is kept securely, is notified to the supplier.

    **(iii)** Outside of production materials and capital expenditure there is no need for higher authority and no cash limit on an individual purchase. In theory this could result in an entire budget being spent inappropriately. All purchases above a certain amount should be authorised by the finance director.

**(c)**

Negotiations by the purchasing manager with suppliers seem to focus only on how long the company can take to pay. There is an opportunity to expand the role of the purchasing manager to (1) guide and authorise budget holders in their purchases and (2) negotiate prices, delivery terms and discounts with existing and new suppliers.

## Task 6.5

**(a)**

There appears to be good co-ordination between ordering and receiving goods, with Goods Inwards expecting receipts since they have the copy orders. They also check the goods before agreeing they are acceptable by signing the documentation and forwarding to accounts so the subsequent invoice can be recorded. These strengths help to ensure that only goods ordered are received, recorded and paid for, and those goods are of acceptable quality. This will help the company's profits.

**(b)**

There is a serious lack of segregation of duties in the accounting function as the same person (the accounts payable clerk) records invoices, asks for credit notes, decides on payment and makes payment. This increases the risk that through collusion or alone, the clerk could engage in fraud, or could make mistakes that are not corrected (especially overpaying, which is unlikely to be complained about by suppliers). At least one other person should be involved in processing, recording, authorising and paying invoices. A third person should be responsible for reviewing figures and procedures.

## Task 6.6

**(a)**

The company maintains a good system of recording and validating production hours spent on individual items of furniture via the job sheets completed by production workers and checked by supervisors. This means the company has a good idea of how much in terms of labour it costs to produce each item, so the company can ensure it covers its costs for each item.

**(b)**

**(i)**    There is no check over signing in and out by production workers. As the payroll clerk prepares wages on the basis of the signing-in book, this means that the company may be paying for hours not worked. In addition the signing-in book should be kept in a secure place and should be checked and authorised by managers/supervisors.

**(ii)**   There is no segregation of duties with regard to payroll accounting, so the payroll clerk may be making mistakes/committing fraud without any checks. In particular the accounts manager should be responsible for authorising amendments to standing data, especially for leavers and joiners, for reviewing the reconciliation of the wages control account, and for authorising or processing bank transfers.

**(c)**

The hours recorded in the signing-in book could be reconciled to the hours of productive work recorded on the job sheets. This would help as a sense check on both records and would also help to identify idle time.

## Task 6.7

| Transaction stream | Risk | Control objective | Control activity |
|---|---|---|---|
| Purchasing | Company pays for goods it does not receive | Ensure all payments are only made for goods actually received, and which are in accordance with the order | Examine goods in for quality and quantity and reconcile the goods to the original order. Issue a goods received note, which is matched to the invoice prior to payment. |
| Sales | Sales recorded late so fines incurred from HMRC with respect to VAT | Record invoices in the correct time period | Implement cut-off procedures. |
| Payroll | Company overpays | Pay employees the correct, authorised gross pay | Refer to standing data when calculating wages and salaries. Implement good timekeeping controls, which are used in the wages calculation. |

## Task 6.8

**(a)**

The original budgeted profit was £73,300 based on budgeted sales of 178,000 units. The actual profit of £80,100 was achieved by selling 192,000 units, some 8% higher sales volume than budgeted.

The original budgeted sales price was £7.20 per unit, while the actual sales price achieved was slightly less at £7.17 per unit.

The main factor leading to the increase in profit was therefore the significant increase in sales volume which more than compensated for the fall in price achieved.

Some categories of costs, eg labour and administration, reported favourable variances in the operating report, which additionally contributed to the increase in profit.

**(b)**

It is possible that there may have been errors in the prices charged to customers. Internal controls over the use of price lists when invoicing, and the completeness of sales recording, should be checked.

Similarly, there may have been errors in processing and recording purchases underlying the costs, or there may have been poor purchasing procedures so that the best deal on prices was not secured.

## Task 6.9

| Transaction stream | Risk | Control objective | Control activity |
|---|---|---|---|
| Payroll | Company incurs fines from HMRC | Ensure all deductions have been properly calculated and authorised | Reconcile total pay and deductions in wages control account regularly. Ensure up-to-date tax codes are used for each employee. |
| Sales | Custom lost through chasing payments already made by the customer | Bank and record all money received accurately | Reconcile the bank account regularly and ensure all receipts are allocated to the correct sales ledger account. |
| Purchasing | Company pays the wrong supplier | Record invoices in the correct purchases ledger account | Reconcile supplier statements with the purchases ledger accounts. |

## Task 6.10

### (a)

Tangible costs are easily identified, quantifiable costs of the change for example buying a new software package. These costs can be calculated based on evidence such as invoices or timesheets. Tangible costs associated with training might include:

- Cost of training course
- Cost of lost chargeable hours (as the staff will not be working on clients' accounts)
- Travel expenses to the training provider

Intangible costs are costs of the change that are more difficult to identify and quantify eg the cost of lost custom as customers go elsewhere during the disruption caused by the change. These might include:

- Other staff feeling discontent as new staff are provided with training which they did not have
- Loss of efficiency as new staff's induction is extended and therefore they are not available for client work
- Client dissatisfaction at delays in completion of work due to staff not being available

### (b) Costs of the system

- Cost of staff time – preparing the data for migration to the new system and assisting the software contractors.
- The cost of the 'learning curve' whereby staff will be slower initially on the new software whilst they practise using it. There may initially be teething problems eg being able to use the reports and understanding what the system can and cannot do.
- Cost of implementing the new system:
    - Full system initial cost £10,800
    - Annual ongoing cost £3,300
- Having an integrated system would lead to reduced calculation errors, simpler and faster online reporting (to HM Revenue and Customs for PAYE) and closer monitoring of the inventory chain.
- Initial training costs will be dependent on how many staff will be trained. If at least 10 staff members (including both directors) are trained, it would be cost effective to have an in-house training programme. The financial outlay would be the same as sending all 10 to college, but it would reduce the travel expenses.

- The downside would be that 10 people would be unavailable to perform business work on the day of training.

- Crachett & Co may consider to send selected members of staff to college to complete the learning, for example five staff members costing £275 each, total cost of £1,375, and these staff could act as 'champions' and assist those members of staff who will complete the online training (such as more restricted users, maybe more junior members of the team or administration or support staff).

- The training programme selected will need to be considered in terms of the financial costs, plus the opportunity costs of staff being unavailable to undertake client work.

- Timing of the change onto the new software would need to be considered as need to think about any downtime from the system, the training time especially in the busy seasons around Christmas and March year ends.

- Staff discontent amongst those not chosen to receive training on the new system. Additionally some staff may get different levels of training, such as some going to college for the course and others completing the online course. This may lower staff morale and productivity.

- Staff completing the online course, there is a risk that they will not complete the training in line with the launch of the new system. The licence allows six months access, so staff using the online training will need to be reviewed to ensure they have completed it on time.

## Workings

Training costs

£2,700 for 15 people is £180 per person

For the same outlay, albeit training people at college, this is £275 per person. Therefore it is cost effective if 10 people at least are trained at the in-house course (£2,700/275 = 9.8).

## Benefits of the system

- Staff are better trained in basic knowledge and skills so they are more efficient.

- Staff morale improves as they feel valued due to the investment in training them, increasing their motivation.

- Customers see well-trained and knowledgeable staff so the company's reputation is enhanced, leading to more repeat custom and recommendations from satisfied customers.

- If everyone is trained at the same time (such as using the in-house training), staff can discuss issues with each other rather than struggling on alone. It will act as a team building exercise and improve morale.

- More efficient working practices, as the bookkeeping, financial reporting and tax reporting will be integrated in the new system, leading to fewer errors and missing information. This could improve profit margins as staff will take less time to complete the client work.

## Conclusion

The partners of Crachett & Co should consider the long term as well as the short term implications of the new software. The new software will enable the firm to become more efficient and also ensuring all updates to the software are completed in a timely manner. Although the costs are initially high (financially and in terms of staff time and effort), the longer term efficiencies and the ability to grow the business will enable Crachett & Co to benefit in the long term.

# BPP PRACTICE ASSESSMENT 1
# LEVEL 4 SYNOPTIC ASSESSMENT

**Time allowed: 3 hours**

**PRACTICE ASSESSMENT 1**

# Level 4 Synoptic Assessment
# BPP practice assessment 1

This practice assessment is based on the same scenario as AAT's sample assessment, SL Products Ltd. See pages 209–214 for the relevant pre-reading material.

## Task 1 (20 marks)

**(a)** **Complete the following statement.**

The statutory duty to report whether SL Products Ltd's financial statements show a true and fair view is that of [                    ▼] .

**Picklist:**

Companies House
Sue Hughes, the chief accountant
the company's directors
the company's auditors

At SL Products Ltd, the duties of processing purchase invoices, purchases ledger and processing payments are separated from each other. Tony Clark, purchasing manager, discovers that a goods returned note has not been followed up by a supplier's accounts department. No credit note has been received or posted to the purchases ledger.

**(2 marks)**

**(b)** **What is the correct action for Tony Clark to take?**

|  | ✓ |
|---|---|
| Prepare a journal to record the necessary reversal of the purchase invoice | |
| Prepare a debit note and send it to the supplier | |
| Advise the accounts payable clerk of the omission | |
| Advise Liz Hall, the accounts payable clerk, to reverse the relevant invoice from the purchases day book | |

**(2 marks)**

(c) **Matthew Tunnock, the accounts receivable clerk, has asked you to show whether the following errors would be detected by reconciling the sales ledger to the sales ledger control account.**

| | |
|---|---|
| VAT on a sales invoice posted to sales instead of VAT control | ▼ |
| A sales invoice credited to the customer's account | ▼ |
| A sales invoice posted to the wrong customer account | ▼ |
| A batch of purchase invoices posted to the sales ledger control account | ▼ |
| A pricing error in a sales invoice | ▼ |

**Picklist:**

Would be detected
Would not be detected

**(5 marks)**

You have been asked to set up an 8-character password for SL Products Ltd's accounting system.

(d) **Which of the following would be the most secure?**

| | ✓ |
|---|---|
| 98765432 | |
| acsystem | |
| 1jan2000 | |
| ?win121# | |

**(2 marks)**

Your duties at SL Products Ltd include running credit checks on new customers. Recently the company has offered a large credit limit to Howlsons Ltd. Its finance director has sent you the following email to thank you for your support:

'Thank you for helping us agree terms of trade with SL Products Ltd. Now that our two companies are connected in this way I trust you will share with me any information you have about BFA Ltd, who also buys from you and who is our biggest competitor.'

**(e) Answer the following questions.**

Which of your fundamental principles is threatened by this request?

| ▼ |
|---|

**Picklist:**

Confidentiality
Objectivity
Professional behaviour

What action should you take?

| ▼ |
|---|

**Picklist:**

You can share some information but must advise BFA Ltd
You must notify the National Crime Agency of the request
You must refuse to share any information

**(4 marks)**

Louise Harding, the Financial Director has asked you to look at the management accounts. She wants you to determine who will be performing the analysis and has asked you to classify the different types of information.

**(f) Identify the type of information provided in the following management reports**

| Wastage reports from the production line | ▼ |
|---|---|
| Inventory turnover reports | ▼ |
| Inventory level reports | ▼ |
| Future demand estimates for the next 12 months | ▼ |
| Analysis of competitor's products and their market positioning | ▼ |

**Picklist:**

Operational
Strategic
Tactical

**(5 marks)**

## Task 2 (15 marks)

SL Products Ltd has a controlling interest in Merville Ltd. Unaudited accounts for Merville Ltd's financial year ended 31 December 20X3 have been prepared and an operating budget for 20X4 has been drafted for approval by the directors of SL Products Ltd.

**You have been asked to review the budget submission by the directors of Merville Ltd.**

---

**Budget submission**

Please find attached our budget proposal for 20X4. Actual (unaudited) results for 20X3 are provided for comparison. Your approval of the budget is requested.

Steady sales growth was achieved in 20X3. During the year we introduced five innovative new products which were quite well-received by the marketplace. All our products are patented in the UK and are therefore protected from direct competition in the UK.

In 20X4, Merville Ltd will continue selling to our own customers and through SL Products Ltd's catalogue. To achieve the targets set for us by our majority shareholder, SL Products Ltd, we also plan to set up and run our own website for selling our products and those of other manufacturers. We aim to start making a great many sales in the EU for the first time.

In total we have 55 products at different stages of their product life cycle. We are in the course of developing three new products. Although it is difficult to achieve raised prices for high-tech products once launched, we hope our new website and the extension of sales into Europe justify a budgeted rise in all our prices, as required by SL Products Ltd. We have therefore budgeted for 10% volume growth in all our products, and approximately 20% revenue growth.

A review of processes in 20X3 means we have been able to start operating more efficiently so we are budgeting for a 2% decrease in costs, again as required by SL Products Ltd.

Overall we are budgeting for a huge increase in the level of profits and the rate of profitability, as required by SL Products Ltd.

---

Product range at start of 20X3: 50. Product range at end of 20X3: 55. New products to be launched in 20X4: 3.

| Operating budget for year ended 31 December 20X4 | Unaudited results 20X3 | Draft budget 20X4 |
|---|---|---|
| Sales volume (units) | 8,500 | 9,350 |
| | £ | £ |
| Sales revenue | 1,239,460 | 1,490,000 |
| Costs: | | |
| Materials | 291,750 | 286,000 |
| Labour | 470,830 | 461,400 |
| Production overheads | 145,030 | 142,100 |
| Depreciation | 52,000 | 51,000 |
| Marketing | 19,500 | 19,100 |
| Administration | 105,420 | 103,300 |
| Total | 1,084,530 | 1,062,900 |
| Operating profit | 154,930 | 427,100 |
| Operating profit % to sales | 12.5% | 28.7% |

**Prepare a report for the chief accountant of SL Products Ltd in three sections as follows:**

(a)  Examine the planning assumptions and calculations in the proposed budget and identify any weaknesses.

(5 marks)

(b)  Evaluate how well the budget would motivate managers to create sustainable, profitable growth.

(5 marks)

**(c)** **Explain how using zero-based budgeting could assist the directors of Merville Ltd.**

**(5 marks)**

## Task 3 (15 marks)

You have been asked to review the adequacy of the control in SL Products Ltd's sales procedures. Your review has established the following information.

The company operates an integrated accounting system which includes a sales accounting module. Cynthia Moss, the Sales Director, is responsible for managing sales activities.

### Ordering and despatch:

- All sales, except those for cash, must be documented on an official customer order. The order should state the agreed price, if known.

- Customer orders must be reviewed and signed by Cynthia Moss.

- Large orders must be signed by Louise Harding, the Finance Director.

- Five copies of the customer order form are printed. Once signed, the original is sent to the customer as an acknowledgement. A copy printed on yellow paper is sent to Matthew Tunnock, the accounts receivable clerk. A pink copy is sent to production and a green copy is sent to despatch. The orange copy is retained by the individual who took the order.

- When the goods are completed, production signs the pink copy and sends it to despatch.

- When the goods are sent out, despatch signs the green copy and sends it, with the pink copy, to Matthew Tunnock.

**New customers:**

- New customers are contacted by Ray Massey, the Credit Controller. He asks for a trade reference and banking details, and offers credit terms.

- He usually offers payment terms as follows:

    - One month from the end of the month in which delivery takes place.
    - With a 5% discount for payment within 21 days of delivery.

    However, terms are subject to negotiation.

**Accounting:**

- All sales invoices are raised by Matthew Tunnock. He matches yellow, pink and green copy orders and prepares the invoices for sending to the customer.

- He posts the invoices to the computerised accounting system.

- He answers queries from customers, issuing credit notes when appropriate.

- Most customers pay by bank transfer. Matthew Tunnock checks the bank account weekly and posts receipts to the ledger accounts.

**Complete your review as follows:**

- **Identify FIVE systemic weaknesses in the company's internal controls for handling sales on credit.**

- **Explain how each weakness that you have identified could create a problem for the company.**

Note. You are **not** required to make recommendations to change procedures.

| No. | Weakness | Potential problem |
|---|---|---|
| | | |
| | | |
| | | |
| | | |
| | | |

**(15 marks)**

## Task 4 (15 marks)

### Review of product pricing

SL Products Ltd has recently suffered a further decline in its gross profit margin. Cynthia Moss (Sales Director) and Louise Harding (Finance Director) are reviewing the situation so they can report to the Board of Directors with proposals to halt the decline.

The market for the company's high-tech products is very competitive, and success depends on constant innovation and better quality than competitor products. After about two years, a product enters the decline phase of its product life-cycle, when there is no scope for price increases and the likelihood of obsolete inventory.

Sue Hughes, the Chief Accountant, proposes that all new products should be priced to give a 25% margin on sales price, to generate as much profit as possible in the early years. She tells you there are two new products that are ready for launch: the AB and the CD.

The company uses a full overhead recovery pricing model. Variable production overheads are equal to 20% of materials and labour, which are all variable.

Cynthia Moss, the sales director, says that Sue's approach to pricing may not be competitive. She has compared each of the two products (AB and CD) with competitors' products and has estimated the sales potential at a price whch gives a 25% margin and one which is designed to be cheaper than competitor prices.

| Price levels and estimated annual volumes | AB | | CD | |
|---|---|---|---|---|
| | £ each | Volume | £ each | Volume |
| Price at 25% margin | To be calculated | 175 | To be calculated | 250 |
| Cheaper than competitor price | 125.00 | 300 | 65.00 | 500 |

Cynthia wants you to calculate which prices would be most profitable.

**(a)** **Complete the following table:**

| Prices for new products | £ per unit | |
|---|---|---|
| | AB | CD |
| Materials and labour | 72.00 | 45.00 |
| Variable production overheads | | |
| Fixed production overheads | 6.00 | 3.00 |
| Other fixed overheads | 6.30 | 3.60 |
| Total cost | | |
| Price at 25% margin | | |
| Marginal cost per unit | | |
| **Annual contribution if price level is...** | | |
| ...price at 25% margin | | |
| ...cheaper than competitor price | | |

**(10 marks)**

**(b)** **Identify factors, other than annual contribution, which are relevant when considering the development and sale of new products.**

**(5 marks)**

## Task 5 (20 marks)

Louise Harding, the Finance Director, is preparing a presentation for the Board of Directors. She has asked you to complete a comparative 'score card' of key financial ratios which she will use as part of her presentation.

Relevant data has been extracted from the last two years' accounts. These extracts do not include the results of Merville Ltd.

| Extracts from accounts of SL Products Ltd | Year ended 31 December 20X2 £000 | Year ended 31 December 20X3 £000 |
| --- | --- | --- |
| Sales revenue | 20,900 | 21,200 |
| Cost of sales | 15,144 | 15,609 |
| Profit from operations | 470 | 328 |
| **Assets** | | |
| Non-current assets | 4,234 | 3,701 |
| Inventories | 3,908 | 4,579 |
| Trade receivables | 3,032 | 3,384 |
| Cash and equivalents | 6 | 8 |
| **Total** | **11,180** | **11,672** |
| **Equity and Liabilities** | | |
| Equity | 5,550 | 5,600 |
| Non-current liabilities | 1,400 | 1,600 |
| Trade payables | 3,730 | 4,020 |
| Bank overdraft | 260 | 302 |
| Tax liabilities | 240 | 150 |
| **Total** | **11,180** | **11,672** |

**(a)** **Complete the scorecard by calculating the missing ratios.**

| SL Products Ltd Scorecard | Year ended 31 Dec 20X2 | Year ended 31 Dec 20X3 |
|---|---|---|
| **Profitability and gearing (correct to 1 dp):** | | |
| Gross profit % | 27.5 % | [          ] % |
| Operating profit % | 2.2 % | [          ] % |
| Return on capital employed | 6.8 % | [          ] % |
| Gearing | 20.1 % | [          ] % |
| **Liquidity ratios (correct to 1 dp):** | | |
| Current ratio | 1.6:1 | [          ] :1 |
| Acid test/quick ratio | 0.7:1 | [          ] :1 |
| **Working capital days (correct to nearest day):** | | |
| Inventory holding period | 94 days | [          ] days |
| Trade receivables collection period | 53 days | [          ] days |
| Trade payables payment period | 90 days | [          ] days |
| Working capital cycle | 57 days | [          ] days |

**(10 marks)**

**(b)** **Select the ONE correct observation about each aspect of business performance below.**

**Profitability**

| | ✓ |
|---|---|
| Profitability has dipped slightly, due to poor sales. | |
| The profitability ratios give serious cause for concern. The small increase in sales revenue has failed to compensate for increased cost of sales and operating expenses. | |

| | ✓ |
|---|---|
| The ratios give mixed messages. Some have improved and some have deteriorated. Further investigation is required. | |

**(2 marks)**

### Gearing

| | ✓ |
|---|---|
| The increased gearing ratio only reflects the fact that an extra loan has been taken out. | |
| The increased gearing ratio shows that equity has increased at a greater rate than non-current liabilities. | |
| The increased gearing ratio shows that the company has become more risky. | |

**(2 marks)**

### Liquidity

| | ✓ |
|---|---|
| Both ratios have deteriorated which indicates that the company is less solvent. | |
| Both ratios have improved, indicating there are no concerns about the company's liquidity or solvency. | |
| The improvement in the liquidity ratios indicates that the company is succeeding in managing its cash flows. | |

**(2 marks)**

### Working capital

| | ✓ |
|---|---|
| The longer working capital cycle indicates the company is insolvent. | |
| The shorter working capital cycle indicates the company can repay some of its long-term liabilities. | |
| The change in the working capital cycle requires urgent investigation. | |

**(2 marks)**

**Overall performance**

| | ✓ |
|---|---|
| Profitability has declined in 20X3, mainly due to competitive pressures. However, the gearing and liquidity measures show an improving financial position. | |
| 20X3 has been a bad year. Profitability has declined and finances are coming under serious pressure. | |
| Steady progress has been made in 20X3. The ratios show that the company is being better managed. | |

**(2 marks)**

## Task 6 (15 marks)

You have been asked to carry out a review of SL Products Ltd's purchases order processing procedure and make recommendations for improvement.

You have interviewed the Finance Director (Louise Harding), the Production Director (Colin Smith) and the Purchasing Manager (Tony Clark). Your findings are below.

- Suppliers are identified and contacted direct by individuals who require the goods or service in question.

- All purchases on credit are recorded on an official purchase order by that individual. The order states the price and delivery date, if known.

- All departments are provided with books of pre-numbered order forms. These books can be obtained from the stationery store.

- Capital expenditure orders must be raised and signed by Louise Harding.

- Other orders must be signed by the individual placing the order.

- New suppliers are given a trade reference and banking details by Tony Clark, who also requests credit terms. These are subject to negotiation, though the company's preferred terms are to pay 60 days from the end of the month in which delivery takes place.

You are required to identify four features of these procedures: one strength; one weakness; one threat and one opportunity. Do not use the same feature more than once.

(a) Identify a strength in these procedures. Explain how the business benefits from the strength.

(3 marks)

(b) Identify a weakness in these procedures. Explain how the weakness damages the business and suggest a remedy.

(4 marks)

**(c)** **Identify an opportunity to improve the procedures to the benefit of the business.**

**(4 marks)**

**(d)** **Identify a threat in these procedures that could damage the business and suggest an action that would reduce the risk.**

**(4 marks)**

# BPP PRACTICE ASSESSMENT 1
# LEVEL 4 SYNOPTIC ASSESSMENT

# ANSWERS

# Level 4 Synoptic Assessment
## BPP practice assessment 1: answers

## Task 1 (20 marks)

**(a)** The statutory duty to report whether SL Products Ltd's financial statements show a true and fair view is that of | the company's auditors | .

**(2 marks)**

**(b)**

|  | ✓ |
|---|---|
| Prepare a journal to record the necessary reversal of the purchase invoice |  |
| Prepare a debit note and send it to the supplier |  |
| Advise the Accounts Payable Clerk of the omission | ✓ |
| Advise Liz Hall, the Accounts Payable Clerk, to reverse the relevant invoice from the purchases day book |  |

**(2 marks)**

**(c)**

| | |
|---|---|
| VAT on a sales invoice posted to sales instead of VAT control | Would not be detected |
| A sales invoice credited to the customer's account | Would be detected |
| A sales invoice posted to the wrong customer account | Would not be detected |
| A batch of purchase invoices posted to the sales ledger control account | Would be detected |
| A pricing error in a sales invoice | Would not be detected |

**(5 marks)**

**(d)**

| | ✓ |
|---|---|
| 98765432 | |
| acsystem | |
| 1jan2000 | |
| ?win121# | ✓ |

**(2 marks)**

**(e)**

| Confidentiality |
|---|

| You must refuse to share any information |
|---|

**(4 marks)**

**(f)**

| | |
|---|---|
| Wastage reports from the production line | Operational |
| Inventory turnover reports | Tactical |
| Inventory level reports | Operational |
| Future demand estimates for the next 12 months | Strategic |
| Analysis of competitor's products and their market positioning | Strategic |

**(5 marks)**

## Task 2 (15 marks)

**(a)**

The draft budget for 20X4 is based on the assumption of 10% growth in sales volume and 20% growth in revenue, despite a decrease of 2% across the board in costs. This appears to be a very ambitious plan which the directors say is justified by the company's expansion into the EU and by the new website. I suggest that we need to:

- Review the market in the EU, which will be much more competitive than the UK as patent protection for the company's products does not extend beyond the UK

- Review the assumptions about the website, in which the company appears to have no experience and for which it does not appear to have budgeted any additional costs (these would appear under Marketing, which shows the same 2% decrease as all other cost categories)

- Review the reasons for the company's declining rate of product innovation (five new products launched in 20X3; only three planned in 20X4) and how the ageing product portfolio affects the growth projection for 20X4

All costs have been decreased by 2% in the draft budget. This takes no account of the volume growth nor the effects of inflation. While it is positive that the review of processes shows scope for efficiency, it seems unlikely that all variable and fixed costs would show the same scope for decrease. In particular, I would expect to see increased marketing spend because of the website and expansion into Europe. Each line of costs needs to be considered carefully according to its cost type (variable, fixed, etc) and its own cost pressures.

**(5 marks)**

**(b)**

The budget does not seem to be realistic. This appears to be because SL Products Ltd has given the directors of Merville Ltd targets for volume and revenue growth, and cost decreases, without involvement in how they can be achieved. Merville Ltd has simply translated these targets into the budget without serious consideration of whether they are realistic or achievable.

Budgetary control can be a powerful tool to encourage managers and staff to create sustainable, profitable growth. To do this, budgets need to be stretching but still achievable.

As the projections for revenue and costs cannot really be achieved they will not help the company either to plan or control its operations in the year ahead. Managers at Merville Ltd will be demotivated by having targets imposed on them which have not been thought through. They will not have 'ownership' of the figures and therefore will not be motivated to achieve them.

I do not believe that this draft budget would motivate Merville Ltd to create sustainable, profitable growth.

**(5 marks)**

**(c)**

Merville Ltd's directors could use zero-based budgeting to review each product and each line of cost in its operations from scratch. This will determine what is realistically achievable for the year ahead. It may be that some costs will no longer be required at all, as suggested by the efficiency review that has already taken place. It might also be that some products will be able to achieve a price rise and volume increases, but not all.

Zero-based budgeting can be a powerful tool for a company to plan and control its operations better in future, though it can be a costly and time-consuming process.

**(5 marks)**

## Task 3 (15 marks)

Marking guide: A maximum of 5 weaknesses and the potential problems, with each weakness awarded 1 mark and each problem 2 marks (to a maximum of 3 marks).

| No. | Weakness | Potential problem |
|-----|----------|-------------------|
| 1 | Cynthia Moss appears to have very little involvement in day to day sales, apart from negotiating terms with new customers. | Failures in the system and system abuses could go unnoticed. |
| 2 | The procedures do not include any mention of checking that goods of the correct category and standard have been despatched. | If this is not happening the company could be sending out sub-standard goods. |
| 3 | Orders can be taken without agreeing a price. | The company is in a weak position to negotiate price after the goods or service have been despatched. |
| 4 | Lack of authorisation of new accounts. | There should be a policy for deciding on whether to offer credit at all. Potential for fraud through collusion with customers. |
| 5 | The terms agreed by Ray Massey are not countersigned. | Potential for fraud through collusion with customers. |
| 6 | Only one signature is required on most orders. | Potential for fraud through collusion with customers. |

| No. | Weakness | Potential problem |
|---|---|---|
| 7 | Matthew Tunnock checks, clears and arranges payment of invoices. | Potential for fraud through collusion with customers. |
| 8 | Matthew Tunnock controls all aspects of sales accounting. | Potential for fraud. |
| 9 | Receipts are only monitored and posted once a week. | Increases the opportunity for teeming and lading, and means a bad service will be given to customers if they ring with a query. |
| 10 | No counter-signatory required for credit notes. | Potential for fraud through collusion with customers. |

**(15 marks)**

**Note.** Only **five** weaknesses were required.

## Task 4 (15 marks)

**(a)**

| Prices for new products | £ per unit | |
|---|---|---|
| | **AB** | **CD** |
| Materials and labour | 72.00 | 45.00 |
| Variable production overheads (W1) | 14.40 | 9.00 |
| Fixed production overheads | 6.00 | 3.00 |
| Other fixed overheads | 6.30 | 3.60 |
| Total cost | 98.70 | 60.60 |
| Price at 25% margin (W2) | 131.60 | 80.80 |
| Marginal cost per unit | 86.40 | 54.00 |
| **Annual contribution if price level is...** | | |
| ...price at 25% margin | 7,910 | 6,700 |
| ...cheaper than competitor price | 11,580 | 5,500 |

### Workings

(1) 20% × materials and labour
(2) Total cost ÷ 0.75

**(b)** It is important to consider other financial and non-financial factors when determining the development and sale of new products, such as:

- How those products fit with other products sold by SL Products and the potential sale of other products in the portfolio

- The availability of cash for the necessary investment into new products, perhaps to finance changes in the production line or expensive advertising campaigns

- The knowledge and skills of staff required to develop and manufacture the products

- Whether there is suffiient payback on any investment given the short life cycle and rate of technological change

- The impact of more technologically advanced products being lauched sooner than anticipated

- The implications in terms of perceived quality of having a price that is lower than competitors

**(5 marks)**

## Task 5 (20 marks)

**(a)**

| SL Products Ltd Scorecard | Year ended 31 Dec 20X2 | Year ended 31 Dec 20X3 |
|---|---|---|
| **Profitability and gearing (correct to 1 dp):** | | |
| Gross profit % | 27.5% | 26.4 % |
| Operating profit % | 2.2% | 1.5 % |
| Return on capital employed | 6.8% | 4.6 % |
| Gearing | 20.1% | 22.2 % |
| **Liquidity ratios (correct to 1 dp):** | | |
| Current ratio | 1.6:1 | 1.8 :1 |
| Acid test/quick ratio | 0.7:1 | 0.8 :1 |

| SL Products Ltd Scorecard | Year ended 31 Dec 20X2 | Year ended 31 Dec 20X3 |
|---|---|---|
| **Working capital days (correct to nearest day):** | | |
| Inventory holding period | 94 days | 107 days |
| Trade receivables collection period | 53 days | 58 days |
| Trade payables payment period | 90 days | 94 days |
| Working capital cycle | 57 days | 71 days |

**(10 marks)**

**(b)  Profitability**

| | ✓ |
|---|---|
| Profitability has dipped slightly, due to poor sales. | |
| The profitability ratios give serious cause for concern. The small increase in sales revenue has failed to compensate for increased cost of sales and operating expenses. | ✓ |
| The ratios give mixed messages. Some have improved and some have deteriorated. Further investigation is required. | |

**(2 marks)**

**Gearing**

| | ✓ |
|---|---|
| The increased gearing ratio only reflects the fact that an extra loan has been taken out. | |
| The increased gearing ratio shows that equity has increased at a greater rate than non-current liabilities. | |
| The increased gearing ratio shows that the company has become more risky. | ✓ |

**(2 marks)**

## Liquidity

| | ✓ |
|---|---|
| Both ratios have deteriorated which indicates that the company is less solvent. | |
| Both ratios have improved, indicating there are no concerns about the company's liquidity or solvency. | |
| The improvement in the liquidity ratios indicates that the company is succeeding in managing its cash flows. | ✓ |

**(2 marks)**

## Working capital

| | ✓ |
|---|---|
| The longer working capital cycle indicates the company is insolvent. | |
| The shorter working capital cycle indicates the company can repay some of its long-term liabilities. | |
| The change in the working capital cycle requires urgent investigation. | ✓ |

**(2 marks)**

## Overall performance

| | ✓ |
|---|---|
| Profitability has declined in 20X3, mainly due to competitive pressures. However, the gearing and liquidity measures show an improving financial position. | |
| 20X3 has been a bad year. Profitability has declined and finances are coming under serious pressure. | ✓ |
| Steady progress has been made in 20X3. The ratios show that the company is being better managed. | |

**(2 marks)**

## Task 6 (15 marks)

**Note.** The question only requires one strength and one weakness. Additional items are provided here to illustrate the range of possible answers.

**(a)**

**(i)** The highest value items – for capital expenditure – require senior management authority before being ordered, and all purchases on credit require proper purchase orders. Staff understand therefore that proper procedures must be followed before items can be purchased, which reduces the risk of unnecessary items being bought by the company or that staff purchase items for themselves at the company's expense.

**(ii)** A coherent approach is taken towards negotiating credit terms with suppliers, which benefits the company's cash flow and planning.

**(3 marks)**

**(b)**

**(i)** It appears items can be purchased from suppliers without a price or delivery time having been agreed upon. This introduces unnecessary uncertainty into the company's operations, costs and cash flows. The remedy is that no purchase orders may be raised without an agreed price being stated on them.

**(ii)** There is no security over the purchase order forms, so in theory any staff member or other person may obtain a form and purchase items to the account of SL Products Ltd. This means the company may be liable to pay for items it has not received or does not want. The remedy is to ensure that purchases can only be recorded and paid for if the purchase invoice when received can be matched to a purchase order.

**(iii)** Outside of capital expenditure there is no need for countersignature to indicate higher authority, and no cash limit on an individual purchase. In theory this could result in large amounts being spent inappropriately.

**(4 marks)**

**(c)**

The involvement of Tony Clark, the Purchasing Manager, with suppliers seems to focus only on how long the company can take to pay. There is an opportunity to expand his role significantly to: (1) identify and quality assure suppliers independently of user departments; (2) guide and authorise departments in their purchases; and (3) negotiate prices, delivery terms and discounts with existing and new suppliers.

**(4 marks)**

**(d)**

The lack of supervision and co-ordination of purchasing suggests that optimum purchasing quantities and careful inventory management are completely overlooked. This could leave the company with significant amounts of inventory that it does not need and cannot use. As well as making a loss on these items, the business will also suffer cash flow problems. There is an urgent need for a more coherent approach to purchasing, especially but not only for Production, so that the company achieves a balance between having inventory when it is needed and having too high a level that drains its resources.

**(4 marks)**

# BPP PRACTICE ASSESSMENT 2
# LEVEL 4 SYNOPTIC ASSESSMENT

**Time allowed: 3 hours**

PRACTICE ASSESSMENT 2

# Level 4 Synoptic Assessment
# BPP practice assessment 2

This practice assessment is based on the same scenario as AAT's sample assessment, SL Products Ltd. See pages 209–214 for the relevant pre-reading material.

## Task 1 (20 marks)

**(a)   Complete the following statement.**

The statutory duty to maintain a public record of information about SL Products Ltd is that of [                    ▼] .

**Picklist:**

Companies House
Sue Hughes, the chief accountant
the company's directors
the company's auditors

At SL Products Ltd the task of preparing the payroll is performed by Jane Patel, Payroll Clerk. Within the company line managers authorise staff timesheets, and Hina Khan (General Accounts Clerk and cashier) processes payments to employees. Colin Smith, Production Director, discovers that the timesheet of the production supervisor, Naseem Hadid, has been omitted from the weekly payroll.

**(2 marks)**

**(b)   What is the correct action for Colin Smith to take?**

|  | ✓ |
|---|---|
| Instruct Hina Khan to make an immediate bank transfer to Naseem |  |
| Advise Jane Patel of the omission |  |
| Prepare a journal to record Naseem's gross pay |  |
| Write out a cheque for Naseem |  |

**(2 marks)**

**(c)** **Jane Patel, the Payroll Clerk, has asked you to show whether the following errors would be detected by clearing the wages control account.**

| | |
|---|---|
| Ten hours pay paid to J. Utley instead of T. Utley | ▼ |
| Gross pay credited to an expense account | ▼ |
| Payment of PAYE to the pension administrator rather than HMRC | ▼ |
| Miscalculation of employer's National Insurance | ▼ |
| A transposition error in the net pay authority given to BACS | ▼ |

**Picklist:**

Would be detected
Would not be detected

**(5 marks)**

You have been asked to ensure the correct controls are in place to validate data input to SL Products Ltd's accounting system.

**(d)** **Which of the following types of control are relevant?**

| | ✓ |
|---|---|
| System controls | |
| Physical access controls | |
| Integrity controls | |

**(2 marks)**

Your duties at SL Products Ltd include preparing the consolidated accounts. Sue Hughes, the chief accountant, is aware that the company's most recent results are not good. She has instructed you to ensure that, when valuing inventory, the highest possible valuation is placed on each item whether or not this is in line with IAS 2 *Inventories*.

**(e)** **Answer the following questions.**

Which of your fundamental principles is threatened by this request?

| ▼ |
|---|

**Picklist:**

Confidentiality
Integrity
Objectivity

What action should you take?

| ▼ |
|---|

**Picklist:**

You must comply with IAS 2 *Inventories*
You must comply with Sue's instruction
You must notify the National Crime Agency of Sue's instruction

**(4 marks)**

**(f)** **Identify whether each of the following control activities is an integrity, system, physical access or management security control. Select your answer using the picklist (answers may be used more than once).**

| | |
|---|---|
| Keypad entry to the accounting office | ▼ |
| User access restrictions to areas of the accountancy software | ▼ |
| Review of the log file for access of areas of the accountancy system by the Financial Director | ▼ |

**Picklist:**

Integrity control
Physical access control
System control

**(3 marks)**

(g) **Which TWO of the following statements reflects a tall organisational structure?**

| | ✓ |
|---|---|
| Management have a wide span of control | |
| Structure is highly dependent on hierarchy | |
| Management do a wide variety of tasks within the organisation | |
| Management have a smaller team, with clear, strict boundaries and tasks set | |

**(2 marks)**

## Task 2 (15 marks)

Cynthia Moss, Sales Director, has performed a review of the products sold by the newly acquired subsidiary Merville Ltd. She has discovered that three products sold are similar. Details of the selling prices and costs of these products are as follows:

| | Product XC72 £ | Product FH54 £ | Product GG44 £ |
|---|---|---|---|
| Selling price per unit | 245 | 225 | 230 |
| Variable costs per unit | | | |
| Materials | 120 | 110 | 70 |
| Labour (@£15/hour) | 30 | 22.50 | 45 |
| Allocated fixed overheads per unit | 25 | 30 | 50 |
| Total cost per unit | 190 | 162.50 | 165 |
| Profit per unit | 70 | 62.50 | 65 |

Cynthia has suggested that Merville should discontinue production of FH54 and GG44 and only produce and sell XC72, as this generates the most profit per unit.

(a)    **Critically evaluate this strategy.**

**(7 marks)**

(b)    **Discuss the impact on your answer if you discover that each of these three products requires the same specialist labour and that it is likely to be in short supply over the next two years.**

**(8 marks)**

## Task 3 (15 marks)

(a) **You have found a number of systemic weaknesses in the internal controls in SL Products Ltd's accounting system. Identify what, if any, effect each one will have on the company's reported profit.**

| Systemic weakness | No effect on reported profit ✓ | Understatement of reported profit ✓ | Overstatement of reported profit ✓ |
|---|---|---|---|
| Omitting sales | | | |
| Understating the allowance for doubtful debts | | | |
| Overstating assets | | | |
| Understating expenses | | | |
| Writing off valid debts as irrecoverable | | | |
| Undervaluation of inventory at the period end | | | |

**(6 marks)**

You have been asked to review the adequacy of the control in SL Products Ltd's payroll procedures. Your review has established the following information.

The company operates an integrated accounting system which includes a payroll accounting module. Sue Hughes, the Chief Accountant, is responsible for managing payroll activities. Jane Patel, the Payroll Clerk, performs day-to-day payroll tasks.

Jane Patel's responsibilities include:

- Maintaining standing data on employees
- Recording each employee's hours at work where this information is relevant and available
- Calculating gross pay and deductions
- Preparing the wages control account

- Preparing the BACS payments each month to employees and HMRC
- Reconciling total pay and deductions in the wages control account

Once a month, after the payroll and its associated payments are complete, Sue Hughes reviews total payroll cost against budget and investigates unexpected variances.

**(b)** **Which THREE of the following types of control activity are weakest in SL Products Ltd's payroll system?**

| | ✓ |
|---|---|
| Physical controls | |
| Segregation of duties | |
| Management controls | |
| Supervisory controls | |
| Organisation | |
| Authorisation (approval) of transactions | |
| Arithmetic and bookkeeping checks | |
| Personnel controls | |

**(3 marks)**

**(c)** **Explain THREE ways in which the weak control activities could create problems for the company.**

Note. You are **not** required to make recommendations to change procedures.

**(i)**

**(ii)**

**(iii)**

**(6 marks)**

........................................................................

## Task 4 (15 marks)

You have been given the following information for the manufacture of units of HW by SL Products Ltd for the month just ended.

|  | Budget | | Actual | |
| --- | --- | --- | --- | --- |
| Production (units of HW) |  | 48,000 |  | 50,400 |
| Direct materials | 19,200 kg | £230,400 | 20,600 kg | £252,350 |

Louise Harding, the Finance Director, has asked you to write a note to help in the training of a junior accounting technician. The notes are to explain the calculation of the total direct material variance and how this variance can be split into a price variance and a usage variance.

**(a)** **Explain the total direct material variance and how it can be split into a price variance and usage variance. Use calculations to illustrate your explanation.**

**(10 marks)**

Sue Hughes, the Chief Accountant, has prepared the following budgetary control report for the product QR produced by SL Products Ltd, together with the variances calculated below.

| | Budget | | Actual | |
|---|---|---|---|---|
| Production (units) | | 5,100 | | 5,500 |
| Direct materials | 15,500 kg | £57,320 | 15,600 kg | £54,600 |
| Direct labour | 10,200 hours | £112,200 | 12,100 hours | £139,150 |
| Fixed overheads | | £97,500 | | £96,300 |
| Total cost | | £267,020 | | £290,050 |

| Variances | Amount £ |
|---|---|
| Direct materials price | 3,090 F |
| Direct materials usage | 4,130 F |
| Direct labour rate | 6,050 A |
| Direct labour efficiency | Not yet calculated |
| Fixed overhead expenditure | Not yet calculated |

SL Products Ltd normally prepares an operating statement under standard absorption costing principles but Louise Harding, the Finance Director, has asked you to prepare an operating statement under standard marginal costing principles.

(b)  Place each variance into the correct column (favourable or
     adverse) and complete the table.

| | | | £ |
|---|---|---|---|
| **Budgeted variable cost for actual production** | | | |
| **Budgeted fixed cost** | | | |
| **Total budgeted cost for actual production** | | | |
| **Variance** | **Favourable £** | **Adverse £** | |
| Direct materials price | | | |
| Direct materials usage | 4,130 | | |
| Direct labour rate | | | |
| Direct labour efficiency | | | |
| Fixed overhead expenditure | | | |
| Fixed overhead volume | | | |
| Total variance | | | 9,730 |
| Actual cost of actual production | | | |

**(5 marks)**

## Task 5 (20 marks)

Louise Harding, the Finance Director, is preparing a presentation for the Board of Directors. She has asked you to complete a comparative 'score card' of key financial ratios which she will use as part of her presentation.

Relevant data has been extracted from the last two years' accounts. These extracts do not include the results of Merville Ltd.

| Extracts from accounts of SL Products Ltd | Year ended 31 December 20X3 £000 | Year ended 31 December 20X4 £000 |
|---|---|---|
| Sales revenue | 21,200 | 23,900 |
| Cost of sales | 15,609 | 15,904 |
| Profit from operations | 328 | 508 |
| **Assets** | | |
| Non-current assets | 3,701 | 4,715 |
| Inventories | 4,579 | 3,197 |
| Trade receivables | 3,384 | 2,559 |
| Cash and equivalents | 8 | 38 |
| **Total** | **11,672** | **10,509** |
| **Equity and Liabilities** | | |
| Equity | 5,600 | 6,200 |
| Non-current liabilities | 1,600 | 1,000 |
| Trade payables | 4,020 | 3,099 |
| Bank overdraft | 302 | 0 |
| Tax liabilities | 150 | 210 |
| **Total** | **11,672** | **10,509** |

(a) **Complete the scorecard by calculating the missing ratios for the year ended 31 December 20X4.**

| SL Products Ltd Scorecard | Year ended 31 Dec 20X3 | Year ended 31 Dec 20X4 |
|---|---|---|
| **Profitability and gearing (correct to 1 dp):** | | |
| Gross profit % | 26.4% | [ ] % |
| Operating profit % | 1.5% | [ ] % |
| Return on capital employed | 4.6% | [ ] % |
| Gearing | 22.2% | [ ] % |
| **Liquidity ratios (correct to 1 dp):** | | |
| Current ratio | 1.8:1 | [ ] :1 |
| Acid test/quick ratio | 0.8:1 | [ ] :1 |
| **Working capital days (correct to nearest day):** | | |
| Inventory holding period | 107 days | [ ] days |
| Trade receivables collection period | 58 days | [ ] days |
| Trade payables payment period | 94 days | [ ] days |
| Working capital cycle | 71 days | [ ] days |

**(10 marks)**

(b) **Select the ONE correct observation about each aspect of business performance below.**

**Profitability**

| | ✓ |
|---|---|
| Profitability has improved due to improved sales and reduced costs. | |
| The profitability ratios have improved due to increased sales, but cost control is still a problem. | |

| | ✓ |
|---|---|
| The ratios give mixed messages. Some have improved and some have deteriorated. Further investigation is required. | |

**(2 marks)**

### Gearing

| | ✓ |
|---|---|
| The reduced gearing ratio reflects that equity has partially replaced lending in the company's financial structure. | |
| The level of gearing is not related to the company's profitability. | |
| The increased gearing ratio shows that the company has become more risky. | |

**(2 marks)**

### Liquidity

| | ✓ |
|---|---|
| Both ratios have deteriorated which indicates that the company is less solvent. | |
| Both ratios have improved, indicating there are no concerns about the company's liquidity or solvency. | |
| Comparing the liquidity ratios with last year's tells us little about the company's solvency. | |

**(2 marks)**

### Working capital

| | ✓ |
|---|---|
| The longer working capital cycle indicates the company is insolvent. | |
| The shorter working capital cycle indicates the company has addressed some solvency issues that appeared in 20X3. | |
| The change in the working capital cycle requires urgent investigation. | |

**(2 marks)**

**Overall performance and position**

| | ✓ |
|---|---|
| The company has a new shareholder whose cash has been used to invest in improving profitability and reducing financial risk. | |
| Steady progress has been made in 20X4, but profitability has declined and the company remains risky. | |
| The company continues to perform badly and is in danger of insolvency. | |

**(2 marks)**

# Task 6 (15 marks)

In the last year SL Products Ltd's subsidiary, Merville Ltd, has found serious weaknesses in each of its three main transaction streams which arise from particular uncontrolled risks. Its finance director has asked you for advice on how to avoid or reduce these risks.

**(a)** **You are required to identify ONE control objective and ONE control activity for each risk.**

| Transaction stream | Risk | Control objective | Control activity |
|---|---|---|---|
| Payroll | Company is fined for non-compliance with PAYE regulations | | |
| Sales | Company charges for goods in error and loses custom | | |
| Purchasing | Company pays more than once for the same goods and the supplier does not correct the mistake | | |

**(6 marks)**

Sue Hughes, the Chief Accountant, presents you with Merville Ltd's monthly operating report. The original budget has been flexed to the level of actual activity, and variances calculated.

You are told that:

- Material, labour and distribution costs are variable.

- Power is a semi-variable cost. The fixed element is budgeted at £5,300 per month.

- Premises costs are stepped, budgeted to double at every 75,000 units of monthly production (at this level the company hires a second workshop at a daily all-inclusive rate).

- Depreciation, marketing and administration costs are fixed.

- The company does not use full absorption costing.

## Monthly operating report

| Original budget | | Flexed budget | Actual | Variance Fav/(Adv) |
|---|---|---|---|---|
| 74,200 | Sales volume (units) | | 80,000 | |
| £ | | £ | £ | £ |
| 534,240 | Sales revenue | 576,000 | 581,400 | 5,400 |
| | Costs | | | |
| 192,920 | Materials | 208,000 | 211,520 | –3,520 |
| 200,340 | Labour | 216,000 | 221,300 | –5,300 |
| 29,680 | Distribution | 32,000 | 33,100 | –1,100 |
| 27,560 | Power | 29,300 | 29,150 | 150 |
| 10,000 | Premises costs | 20,000 | 10,000 | 10,000 |
| 3,650 | Depreciation | 3,650 | 3,600 | 50 |
| 32,500 | Marketing | 32,500 | 33,400 | –900 |
| 10,670 | Administration | 10,670 | 9,980 | 690 |
| 507,320 | Total | 552,120 | 552,050 | 70 |
| | | | | |
| 26,920 | Operating profit/(loss) | 23,880 | 29,350 | 5,470 |

**Write an email to Sue Hughes to explain:**

**(b)** The main factors that led to the actual profit being higher than the original budgeted profit.

**(5 marks)**

**(c)** How improved internal controls can assist in controlling the adverse variances.

**(4 marks)**

# BPP PRACTICE ASSESSMENT 2
# LEVEL 4 SYNOPTIC ASSESSMENT

# ANSWERS

# Level 4 Synoptic Assessment
# BPP practice assessment 2: answers

## Task 1 (20 marks)

**(a)** The statutory duty to maintain a public record of information about SL Products Ltd is that of ⌊Companies House⌋ .

**(2 marks)**

**(b)**

| | ✓ |
|---|---|
| Instruct Hina Khan to make an immediate bank transfer to Naseem | |
| Advise Jane Patel of the omission | ✓ |
| Prepare a journal to record Naseem's gross pay | |
| Write out a cheque for Naseem | |

**(2 marks)**

**(c)**

| | |
|---|---|
| Ten hours pay paid to J. Utley instead of T. Utley | Would not be detected |
| Gross pay credited to an expense account | Would be detected |
| Payment of PAYE to the pension administrator rather than HMRC | Would not be detected |
| Miscalculation of employer's National Insurance | Would not be detected |
| A transposition error in the net pay authority given to BACS | Would be detected |

**(5 marks)**

**(d)**

| | ✓ |
|---|---|
| System controls | |
| Physical access controls | |
| Integrity controls | ✓ |

**(2 marks)**

**(e)**

| Integrity |
| --- |

| You must comply with IAS 2 *Inventories* |
| --- |

**(4 marks)**

**(f)**

| | |
| --- | --- |
| Keypad entry to the accounting office | Physical access control |
| User access restrictions to areas of the accountancy software | Integrity control |
| Review of the log file for access of areas of the accountancy system by the Financial Director | System control |

**(3 marks)**

**(g)**

| | ✓ |
| --- | --- |
| Management have a wide span of control | |
| Structure is highly dependent on hierarchy | ✓ |
| Management do a wide variety of tasks within the organisation | |
| Management have a smaller team, with clear, strict boundaries and tasks set. | ✓ |

**(2 marks)**

## Task 2 (15 marks)

**(a)**

The objective of companies is to maximise profit so, at first sight, the decision to focus on the product which generates most profit seems quite sensible.

However the profit per unit is calculated after deducting the fixed overheads which have been allocated to each product. The allocation to individual products is inevitably arbitrary, as the overheads do not relate to a particular product type. We are not told how fixed overheads have been allocated to individual products, but a change in the method of overhead allocation could produce very different amounts for profit per unit.

A better decision-making rule is to try to maximise contribution, which is achieved by focussing on the product with the highest contribution per unit. Contribution per unit is selling price per unit minus variable costs. Each unit sold contributes this amount towards paying the fixed costs and maximising total contribution which will ultimately generate more profit regardless of how fixed costs are allocated.

The contribution per unit of the three products are £95 (£245 – £150), £92.50 (£225 – £132.50) and £115 (£230 – £115) respectively. This would suggest that, if Merville is to restrict production to one product, it should only produce and sell GG44.

However there are further issues to consider. If XC72 and FH54 are discontinued, then the fixed overheads allocated to those products would need to be covered elsewhere. Sales of GG44 would be expected to increase so presumably more overhead would be absorbed by these sales, but there may be implications for the total (absorption) costs of a variety of other products sold by Merville.

Also, it is not a given that customers would be happy to buy GG44 instead of XC72 and FH54. Just because these products are similar does not mean that they are identical, and GG44 sells for £5 more than FH54. Merville may lose more revenue (and therefore contribution) than it gains.

In conclusion, Merville should not rush into this decision as it may not be as straightforward as it first appears.

**(7 marks)**

**(b)**

In situations where there is a limiting factor, such as labour in this case, the decision rule changes. Merville should aim to maximise contribution per unit of limiting factor, which in this case would be contribution per labour hour as this will in turn maximise profit.

Cynthia should therefore calculate contribution per unit divided by number of hours of labour required to produce each unit. As we know labour is £15 per hour, this means that contributions per labour hour are £47.50 (£95/2), £61.70 (£92.50/1.5) and £38.30 (£115/3) respectively. This would suggest that, if Merville intends to pursue its one-product strategy, it should concentrate on FH54. As FH54 uses half the labour of GG44, Merville can produce twice as many of FH54 with the available labour.

However the points made about overhead allocation and product substitution in a one-product strategy remain valid.

**(8 marks)**

## Task 3 (15 marks)

**(a)**

| Systemic weakness | No effect on reported profit ✓ | Understatement of reported profit ✓ | Overstatement of reported profit ✓ |
|---|---|---|---|
| Omitting sales | | ✓ | |
| Understating the allowance for doubtful debts | | | ✓ |
| Overstating assets | ✓ | | |
| Understating expenses | | | ✓ |
| Writing off valid debts as irrecoverable | | ✓ | |
| Undervaluation of inventory at the period end | | ✓ | |

**(6 marks)**

**(b)**

| | ✓ |
|---|---|
| Physical controls | |
| Segregation of duties | ✓ |
| Management controls | |
| Supervisory controls | ✓ |
| Organisation | |
| Authorisation (approval) of transactions | ✓ |
| Arithmetic and bookkeeping checks | |
| Personnel controls | |

**(3 marks)**

**(c)**

**(i)** The chief accountant appears to have nothing to do with day-to-day payroll activities, only exercising a light level of management control by reviewing actual payroll costs against budget after payments to employees and HMRC have been processed. Errors or even fraud could easily take place in Jane Patel's work without any early warning system for SLP's management.

**(ii)** The lack of segregation of duties in the payroll system means that there are no day-to-day checks and balances on Jane Patel's work, so the company is wide open to both misappropriation and misstatement. Through collusion with others or acting alone, Jane could create fictitious employees, fail to remove leavers from the payroll, misreport hours to be paid, miscalculate gross pay and deductions, make recording and posting errors, and make over- or under-payments of net pay to employees.

**(iii)** The lack of authorisation of transactions means that intentional frauds or unintentional errors could pass unnoticed, and the company could pay for hours that have not been worked.

**(6 marks)**

## Task 4 (15 marks)

(a)

The total direct material variance compares the **flexed budget cost** for materials with the **actual cost** incurred. The flexed budget is the total budgeted cost of materials for the actual production of 50,400 units. It is not useful simply to calculate the variance as £21,950 adverse by comparing the actual cost of £252,350 with the budgeted cost of £230,400, because the two figures are based on different volumes of activity.

Flexing the budget calculates the **quantity of materials** which we would expect to use to produce the **actual production** achieved. If 19,200 kgs are required to make 48,000 units then 0.4 kg is required to make 1 unit (19,200/48,000). To make 50400 units we therefore require 20,160 kgs (50,400 × 0.4 kg). We expect each kg to cost £12 (£230,400/19,200). Therefore we expect that making 50,400 units would require 20,160 kilograms at a cost of £12 per kilogram, that is £241,920.

We now compare the **flexed budget cost** of £241,920 with the **actual cost** (£252,350) to produce the total material variance of £10,430. This variance is adverse because the **actual cost was greater than the flexed budgeted cost**.

The total variance can be split into two elements:

- The variance due to the price paid per kilogram being different to what we expected. This is the material price variance.

- The variance due to the quantity of material used per unit of production being different to what we expected. This is the material usage variance.

The expected cost of the 20,600 kilograms used is £247,200 (20,600 × £12).

### Price variance

We calculate the price variance by comparing the **actual cost** of the 20,600 kilograms (£252,350) with the **expected cost** (£247,200). The difference or variance is £5,150. This variance is adverse because the **actual cost is greater than the expected cost**.

### Material usage variance

We calculate the material usage variance by calculating the quantity of materials which we would expect to use to produce the actual volume of production. 50,400 units were produced and the expected quantity of materials to make these units is 20,160 kilograms. If we compare this to the actual quantity used of 20,600 kilograms we get an adverse variance of 440 kilograms, since we used more than we expected. This needs to be **valued at the expected cost** of £12 per kilogram. The adverse usage

variance is £5,280 (440 × £12). The usage variance is always valued at the expected cost (the standard cost) because the price variance has already been isolated.

**Total materials variance**

Together the materials price and usage variances reconcile back to the total materials variance. The price variance of £5,150 adverse plus the £5,280 adverse usage variance explains the total variance of £10,430.

**(10 marks)**

**(b)**

| | | | £ |
|---|---|---|---|
| **Budgeted variable cost for actual production** | | | 182,820 |
| **Budgeted fixed cost** | | | 97,500 |
| **Total budgeted cost for actual production** | | | 280,320 |

| Variance | Favourable £ | Adverse £ | |
|---|---|---|---|
| Direct materials price | 3,090 | | |
| Direct materials usage | 4,130 | | |
| Direct labour rate | | 6,050 | |
| Direct labour efficiency | | 12,100 | |
| Fixed overhead expenditure | 1,200 | | |
| Fixed overhead volume | | | |
| Total variance | 8,420 | 18,150 | 9,730 |
| Actual cost of actual production | | | 290,050 |

**(5 marks)**

**Workings**

Budgeted variable cost per unit = (£57,320 + £112,200)/5,100 units = £33.24

Budgeted variable cost for actual production = 5,500 units × £33.24 = £182,820

Total budgeted cost for actual production = £182,820 + £97,500 (fixed costs)

= £280,320

Direct labour efficiency variance

| 5,500 units should have taken (× 10,200/5,100 hours) | 11,000 hrs |
|---|---|
| But did take | 12,100 hrs |
|  | 1,100 hrs (A) |
| At standard rate (£112,200/10,200) | × £11.00 |
| Efficiency variance | £12,100 (A) |

Fixed overhead expenditure variance = £97,500 − £96,300 = £1,200. Actual £1,200 lower than budgeted, so favourable.

## Task 5 (20 marks)

**(a)**

| SL Products Ltd Scorecard | Year ended 31 Dec 20X3 | Year ended 31 Dec 20X4 |
|---|---|---|
| **Profitability and gearing (correct to 1 dp):** | | |
| Gross profit % | 26.4% | 33.5 % |
| Operating profit % | 1.5% | 2.1 % |
| Return on capital employed | 4.6% | 7.1 % |
| Gearing | 22.2% | 13.9 % |
| **Liquidity ratios (correct to 1 dp):** | | |
| Current ratio | 1.8:1 | 1.8 :1 |
| Acid test/quick ratio | 0.8:1 | 0.8 :1 |
| **Working capital days (correct to nearest day):** | | |
| Inventory holding period | 107 days | 73 days |
| Trade receivables collection period | 58 days | 39 days |
| Trade payables payment period | 94 days | 71 days |
| Working capital cycle | 71 days | 41 days |

**(10 marks)**

**(b)** **Profitability**

| | ✓ |
|---|---|
| Profitability has improved due to improved sales and reduced costs. | ✓ |
| The profitability ratios have improved due to increased sales, but cost control is still a problem. | |
| The ratios give mixed messages. Some have improved and some have deteriorated. Further investigation is required. | |

**(2 marks)**

**Gearing**

| | ✓ |
|---|---|
| The reduced gearing ratio reflects that equity has partially replaced lending in the company's financial structure. | ✓ |
| The level of gearing is not related to the company's profitability. | |
| The increased gearing ratio shows that the company has become more risky. | |

**(2 marks)**

**Liquidity**

| | ✓ |
|---|---|
| Both ratios have deteriorated which indicates that the company is less solvent. | |
| Both ratios have improved, indicating there are no concerns about the company's liquidity or solvency. | |
| Comparing the liquidity ratios with last year's tells us little about the company's solvency. | ✓ |

**(2 marks)**

## Working capital

| | ✓ |
|---|---|
| The longer working capital cycle indicates the company is insolvent. | |
| The shorter working capital cycle indicates the company has addressed some solvency issues that appeared in 20X3. | ✓ |
| The change in the working capital cycle requires urgent investigation. | |

**(2 marks)**

## Overall performance and position

| | ✓ |
|---|---|
| The company has a new shareholder whose cash has been used to invest in improving profitability and reducing financial risk. | ✓ |
| Steady progress has been made in 20X4, but profitability has declined and the company remains risky. | |
| The company continues to perform badly and is in danger of insolvency. | |

**(2 marks)**

# Task 6 (15 marks)

## (a)

| Transaction stream | Risk | Control objective | Control activity |
|---|---|---|---|
| Payroll | Company is fined for non-compliance with PAYE regulations | Ensure all deductions have been properly calculated and authorised | Check calculation and authorisation of all deductions<br><br>Maintain separate records for each employee<br><br>Reconcile total pay and deductions in wages control account regularly |
| Sales | Company charges for goods in error and loses custom | Only invoice goods that have been sent out | Ask customers to sign despatch notes as proof of receipt<br><br>Prepare sales invoices from signed despatch notes and sales orders |
| Purchasing | Company pays more than once for the same goods and the supplier does not correct the mistake | Only pay for liabilities once | Record payments promptly in the cash book and ledger. Only pay supplier invoices that match checked GRNs |

**(6 marks)**

**(b)**

The key factor leading to the actual profit being higher than the originally budgeted profit is the increase in sales volume achieved. Actual sales were 80,000 units compared to an original budget of 74,200 units, an 8% increase. Also helping is an increase in the sales price achieved, budgeted to be £534,240/74,200 = £7.20 per unit, but actually achieved at £581,400/80,000 = £7.27, a 0.9% increase.

The second reason for the higher than budgeted profit is the £10,000 favourable variance on premises costs. A second workshop was budgeted but the company has managed with one workshop, presumably because opening inventory of finished goods was sufficient to achieve sales of 80,000 units without producing more than 75,000 units in the year.

Some costs, eg materials and labour, report adverse variances so tend to reduce the profit achieved. Others, eg administration, report a favourable variance so increase the profit achieved.

However it is the favourable increase in sales volume and premises variances that are the main factors in explaining the increase in profit.

**(5 marks)**

**(c)**

It is possible that there may have been errors in the prices charged by suppliers for materials and distribution. Internal controls over the use of price lists when ordering should be checked. There may have been errors in processing and recording purchases underlying the costs, or there may have been poor purchasing procedures so that the best deal on prices was not secured.

As far as labour costs are concerned there may be operational reasons, such as the use of overtime, for the variance on labour costs. However, there may have been poor control of time, mis-recording of time, and deliberate or careless overpayment of employees. Authorisation and management controls over payroll costs should be reviewed.

**(4 marks)**

# AAT AQ2016 PRACTICE ASSESSMENT 1
# LEVEL 4 SYNOPTIC ASSESSMENT

**Time allowed: 3 hours**

AAT AQ2016

PRACTICE ASSESSMENT 1

# Level 4 Synoptic Assessment
## AAT practice assessment 1

## Company background and history

SL Products Ltd (SLP) is a market-leading manufacturing business supplying advanced technological electronics to a number of companies around the world.

The company operates through a manufacturing division and a sales division. The manufacturing division supplies electronics to the sales division, which sells both its own manufactured product and other complementary products that it buys in from third parties.

SLP has its head office on an industrial estate in Manchester, where its management team and accounts department are both based. Its main manufacturing plant is also on this site, as is the sales division's offices and large central warehouse.

SLP was established 10 years ago by three of its four controlling shareholders, Shaun Murphy, Colin Smith and Cynthia Moss. Six years ago they sold most of their shareholding in the business, and now do not have a controlling interest.

Louise Harding was brought into the company and joined the board as Finance Director just over 18 months ago when the other directors and main shareholders realised the company's urgent need to have more high-level professional accounting expertise.

Over the past 10 years, the company has grown rapidly and in the year ended 31 December 20X1 it had a turnover of £20 million. It also now employs around 400 full-time equivalent employees. However, profits from operations have fallen in recent years.

In an attempt to improve profitability, SLP has recently acquired a controlling interest in Merville Ltd, a small manufacturing business that offers unique, patented products that are complementary to those manufactured by SLP. Merville Ltd has prepared initial accounts for its first year of trading under the control of SLP.

A management bonus is linked to these results but it has not yet been authorised for payment by SLP's remuneration committee.

## SLP's mission statement

We aim to be a market-focused business that specialises in the research, manufacture and distribution of passive electronic components.

Our priorities are quality, service and providing a product range at the cutting-edge of technology. We offer our customers cost effective products of the highest quality.

We aim to develop long-term relationships with all our stakeholders and deal with suppliers, customers and our staff with the highest levels of integrity.

## Developments in the electronics market

During the past few years, the company has been feeling the effects of a recession. Intense competition from overseas manufacturers, made worse by the strength of the pound, has led to a progressive lowering of market prices within the areas in which SLP operates.

It is also becoming increasingly difficult for small companies like SLP to compete with the Research and Development (R&D) budgets available to larger businesses. As the pace of technological change in electronics has accelerated, the company's product range has gradually lost the lead it once had in cutting-edge technology.

The directors have now reluctantly decided that they may be forced to downsize some parts of the business that they spent the past 10 years building up. On the other hand, as they are unable to outspend their bigger competitors on R&D, they are looking to acquire stakes in companies like Merville Ltd to fill the resulting gaps in their product range.

## SLP's strategic planning and control

When Louise Harding joined SLP, she suggested that they need to view it from different perspectives rather than just focus on its financial results. The directors and the controlling shareholders agreed to develop measures, collect data and judge the company's performance relative to each of these perspectives. These measures have now been in place for a full year and have just been reviewed.

## Perspective 1

The first perspective involves employee training and having corporate cultural attitudes that relate to both individual and corporate self-improvement. In an organisation, such as SLP, that relies on problem solving and creative thinking, its people are an important resource. In a market characterised by rapid technological change, it is necessary for staff to be in a continuous learning mode.

Measures were put into place to focus training and development funds where they could help the most.

This perspective, which recognises that 'learning' is more than 'training', also considers aspects such as the effectiveness of mentoring within the organisation, as well as the ease of communication among workers that allows them to get help with a problem easily, when needed.

In general, the first year's results show that the company has performed well in relation to this perspective.

## Perspective 2

The second perspective refers to internal business processes. Measures based on this perspective allow the directors to see how well their business is running, and

whether its products and services conform to customer requirements (as per its mission statement).

Those who know these processes most intimately, namely the various line managers within SLP, carefully designed these measures.

In general, the first year's results show that the company has performed poorly in relation to this perspective. This is because the business is gradually losing its technological lead in several of its products.

## Perspective 3

The third perspective relates to how SLP's customers view the business. Cynthia Moss has stressed the importance of customer focus and customer satisfaction. She has emphasised that these are leading indicators; if customers are not satisfied, they will eventually find other suppliers that will meet their needs better. Poor performance on this perspective is therefore a key indicator of future decline, even though the current financial results may still look reasonable.

To develop measures for customer satisfaction, SLP examined its customers both in terms of the kinds of customers they are, and the kinds of products that they are buying from SLP.

The first year's results indicate that customers were generally satisfied with the customer care and service, but were less satisfied with some of the older products in the product range that were overdue for replacement.

Interestingly, customers were generally more satisfied with the bought-in products being sold by the sales division than those manufactured in-house by SLP itself. There was considerable interest in the new products manufactured by Merville Ltd.

## Perspective 4

The fourth and final perspective is the traditional outlook using financial data. Louise Harding instigated the use of more accurate and timely monthly management accounts immediately after she was appointed. She argued that the previous focus on only financial data had led to an 'unbalanced' situation with no attention having been paid to the real drivers of business performance.

The financial results continue to show falling profits which the other three perspectives help to explain.

## Strategy-mapping

SLP has used the first year's results to carry out a strategy-mapping exercise (strategy maps are communication tools used to tell a story of how value is created for the organisation. They show a logical, step-by-step connection between strategic objectives in the form of causes and effects).

Generally speaking, improving performance in the objectives from the first of SLP's perspectives will enable it to improve its internal processes. This will enable it to

improve its results for customer satisfaction and eventually its financial performance.

This implies that SLP needs to reallocate resources towards increasing its R&D spend which will, in turn, redirect its internal processes towards new product development. This should result in improved customer satisfaction and retention, with the final outcome being increased profitability.

Some of the directors, however, believe that the root cause of SLP's problems lies in exactly the matters that are under the Finance Director's direct control, ie the problems are due to poor internal controls and systemic weaknesses. The directors also point out that they will struggle to finance any increase in R&D.

At this point in time, the board is divided and uncertain how best to proceed.

### Staff

SLP's key personnel are as follows:

| | |
|---|---|
| **Managing director** | Shaun Murphy |
| **Finance director** | Louise Harding |
| **Production director** | Colin Smith |
| **Sales director** | Cynthia Moss |
| **Chief accountant** | Sue Hughes |
| **Purchasing manager** | Tony Clark |
| **Warehouse manager** | Robert Utley |
| **Credit controller** | Ray Massey |
| **Accounts payable clerk** | Liz Hall |
| **Accounts receivable clerk** | Matthew Tunnock |
| **General accounts clerk and cashier** | Hina Khan |
| **Payroll clerk** | Jane Patel |

### SLP's financial statements

The financial statements for SLP for the year ended 31 December 20X1 show that the company had a turnover of £20 million, and made a profit after tax of £960,000.

These accounts do not include the results of Merville Ltd, which was acquired on 1 January 20X2.

## SL Products Ltd – Statement of profit or loss for the year ended 31 December 20X1

| Continuing operations | £000 |
| --- | --- |
| **Revenue** | 20,000 |
| Cost of sales | (14,322) |
| Gross profit | 5,678 |
| Operating expenses | (4,413) |
| **Profit from operations** | 1,265 |
| Finance costs | (47) |
| **Profit before tax** | 1,218 |
| **Tax** | (258) |
| **Profit for the period from continuing operations** | 960 |

## SL Products Ltd – Statement of financial position as at 31 December 20X1

| | £000 |
| --- | --- |
| **ASSETS** | |
| **Non-current assets** | |
| Property, plant and equipment | 4,330 |
| | 4,330 |
| **Current assets** | |
| Inventories | 3,614 |
| Trade receivables | 2,976 |
| Cash and cash equivalents | 8 |
| | 6,598 |
| **Total assets** | 10,928 |

| | £000 |
|---|---|
| **EQUITY AND LIABILITIES** | |
| **Equity** | |
| Ordinary share capital (£1 shares) | 800 |
| Share premium | 1,160 |
| Retained earnings | 4,065 |
| **Total equity** | 6,025 |
| **Non-current liabilities** | |
| Bank loans | 1,200 |
| | 1,200 |
| **Current liabilities** | |
| Trade payables | 3,360 |
| Bank overdraft | 124 |
| Tax liabilities | 219 |
| | 3,703 |
| **Total liabilities** | 4,903 |
| **Total equity and liabilities** | 10,928 |

## Task 1 (20 marks)

Louise Harding, the Finance Director of SL Products Ltd has asked you to analyse the published results of a competitor business. Until recently, you were employed by that business. Therefore, you have a detailed understanding of its financial position.

**(a)** **Answer the following questions.**

**Which of your principles is threatened by this request?**

**Picklist:**

Confidentiality
Objectivity
Professional competence and due care

**How should you respond?**

[               ▼ ]

**Picklist:**

Base your analysis entirely on the published results
Obtain the competitor's agreement
Refuse to do the analysis

**(4 marks)**

Hina Khan, the Cashier of SL Products Ltd, is preparing a cash flow forecast. She asks which of the following are cash flow items.

**(b)** **Show whether each of the following should be included in a cash flow forecast by selecting your answers from the picklist.**

Revaluation of premises

[               ▼ ]

Bonus issue of shares in SL Products Ltd

[               ▼ ]

Payment of dividend on ordinary shares

[               ▼ ]

Write off obsolete inventory

[               ▼ ]

**Picklist:**

Do not include
Include in cash flow

**(8 marks)**

Liz Hall, the Accounts Payable Clerk, asks for you for advice. She wants to know whether the following errors and discrepancies would be detected by reconciling the accounts payable ledger to its control account.

**(c)** **Show whether each of the following errors and discrepancies would be detected by reconciling the accounts payable ledger to its control account by selecting your answers from the picklist.**

| Errors and discrepancies | Answer |
|---|---|
| A supplier has been paid for an invoice twice | ▼ |
| A supplier invoice has been posted to the wrong supplier account | ▼ |
| A cheque payment has been debited to the accounts receivable control account | ▼ |
| VAT on some purchases has been omitted from the VAT return | ▼ |
| A purchase invoice has been debited to the account of a supplier | ▼ |

**Picklist:**

Would be detected
Would not be detected

**(5 marks)**

Liz Hall maintains the accounts payable ledger. Her duties include ensuring the accounts payable ledger agrees to its control account.

**(d)   What sort of access should Liz have to the accounts payable control account?**

**Picklist:**

Full access, including data entry
No access
Read only access

**(1 mark)**

An inventory count is to take place at SL Products Ltd's financial year end. Sue Hughes, Chief Accountant, is concerned that the inventory value will appear to be too high. She suggests that all inventory receipts in the final week of December should be dated 1 January and that those items should be excluded from the count. The relevant purchase invoices would be posted in the new accounting period.

**(e)** **Which of the following statements describes this suggestion?**

|  | ✓ |
| --- | --- |
| Acceptable commercial practice |  |
| Unethical 'window dressing' |  |
| Fraud |  |
| Breach of the control environment |  |

**(2 marks)**

## Task 2 (15 marks)

SL Products Ltd acquired a controlling interest in a small manufacturing business called Merville Ltd on 1 January 20X2.

Unaudited accounts for Merville Ltd's financial year ended 31 December 20X2 have been prepared and an operating budget has been drafted for approval by the directors of SL Products Ltd.

The administration costs for 20X2 include a provision of £21,000 for a profit related management bonus, payable to the directors of Merville Ltd.

**You have been asked to review the budget proposal and supporting submission.**

**Budget submission**

The directors of Merville Ltd are pleased to present a budget proposal for 20X3. Actual (unaudited) results for 20X2 are provided for comparison. Your approval of the budget is requested.

Substantial sales growth was achieved in 20X2. We introduced more than a dozen innovative new products. The key features of these products are patented and therefore protected for direct competition. Merville Ltd has a solid customer base.

In 20X3, Merville Ltd will retain its own identity in the market place. In addition, we plan to develop a sales channel through SL Products Ltd and to be promoted in that company's catalogue.

We have 50 products in our catalogue at all stages of the product life cycle. More exciting new products are being planned. We do not feel that it is realistic to try to calculate sales revenue and costs at product level. However, we are confident that we will achieve the budgeted 10% volume growth.

We have not assumed any increase in selling prices because this is difficult to achieve with high-tech products.

In addition to the 10% volume growth, we have allowed 2.5% for cost increases in line with expected inflation.

| Operating budget for year ended 31 December 20X3 | Unaudited results 20X2 | Draft budget 20X3 |
|---|---|---|
| Sales volume (units) | 7,950 | 8,745 |
| | £ | £ |
| Sales revenue | 1,128,900 | 1,241,790 |
| Costs: | | |
| Materials | 246,450 | 277,256 |
| Labour | 409,425 | 460,603 |
| Production overheads | 144,690 | 162,776 |
| Depreciation | 46,800 | 52,650 |
| Marketing | 18,640 | 20,970 |
| Administration | 92,600 | 104,175 |
| Total | 958,605 | 1,078,430 |
| Operating profit | 170,295 | 163,360 |
| Operating profit % to sales | 15.1% | 13.2% |

**Prepare a report for the chief accountant of SL Products Ltd in three sections as follows:**

**(a)  Examine the planning assumptions and calculations in the proposed budget and identify any weaknesses.**

**(5 marks)**

**(b)** **Explain how costs and profitability should be managed in an organisation that manufactures multiple products.**

**(5 marks)**

**(c)** **Give your opinion, with reasons, on how well the budget would motivate managers to create sustainable, profitable growth.**

**(5 marks)**

## Task 3 (15 marks)

You have been asked to review the adequacy of the control in SL Products Ltd's purchasing procedures. Your review has established the following information.

The company operates an integrated accounting system which includes a purchase accounting module. Tony Clark, the Purchasing Manager, is responsible for managing purchasing activities.

**Ordering and receipt:**

- All purchases, except petty cash items, must be documented on an official purchase order. The order should state the agreed price, if known.

- All departments are provided with books of pre-numbered order forms. These books can be obtained from the stationery store.

- Orders for production materials and items for resale must be signed by Robert Utley, the warehouse manager.

- Capital expenditure orders must be signed by Louise Harding, the finance director.

- There is no cash limit for purchase orders provided that they are within the approved budget.

- Other orders must be signed by the relevant budget holders.

- Four copies of the order form are printed. Once signed, the original is sent to the supplier. A copy printed on yellow paper is sent to Liz Hall, the accounts payable clerk. Two further copies, printed on pink and green paper, are retained by the individual who raised the order.

- When the goods or service(s) are received, the individual who raised the order signs the green copy and sends it to Liz Hall. This individual retains the pink copy for their files.

**New suppliers:**

- New suppliers are contacted by Tony Clark. He provides a trade reference and banking details and requests credit terms.

- He usually requests payment terms as either of the following:

  - Two months from the end of the month in which delivery takes place
  - A 5% discount for payment within 21 days of delivery

  However, terms are subject to negotiation.

- Tony enters the agreed supplier details and payment terms into the supplier master file.

**Accounting:**

- All purchase invoices are checked by Liz Hall. She checks the calculations, matches the invoices to appropriate yellow and green copy orders and clears the invoices for payment.

- Liz posts the cleared invoices to the computerised accounting system.

- Liz takes up queries with suppliers, requesting credit notes when appropriate.

- Invoices are automatically paid as they fall due through the bankers automated clearing system (BACS). Liz authorises one payment run every week.

**Complete your review as follows, using the provided answer spaces below:**

- **Identify FIVE systemic weaknesses in the company's internal controls for handling purchases on credit.**
- **Explain how each weakness that you have identified could create a problem for the company.**

**Note.** You are **not** required to make recommendations to change procedures.

| No. | Weakness | Potential problem |
|---|---|---|
| | | |
| | | |
| | | |
| | | |
| | | |

**(15 marks)**

## Task 4 (15 marks)

### Review of product pricing

The latest annual results of SL Products Ltd have confirmed the trend of decline in the gross profit margin. The Board of Directors has asked Cynthia Moss (Sales Director) and Louise Harding (Finance Director) to review the situation and report back with an agreed proposal.

The company operates in a very competitive, high-tech market. It is necessary to create a stream of innovative new products that are as good as, or better than, those marketed by competitors. Meanwhile, older products rapidly go into decline. It is almost impossible to increase the price of a product after it is launched.

Louise proposes that all new products should be priced to give a 30% mark-up over cost. She says, 'we only get one chance to get the price right. Production costs are always rising but we cannot increase our prices. If we launch the products with a 30% mark-up, they will be profitable for a few years.'

Sue Hughes, the chief accountant, has created a simple spreadsheet model to determine the selling prices for new products. She has used this model to calculate the selling price of two new products that are ready for launch.

### Pricing spreadsheet

Sue explains that this is a full overhead recovery pricing model.

The variable element of production overheads is equal to 15% of the direct costs. (The direct costs are all variable.) Marketing and administration costs are fixed.

| Prices for new products | £ per unit | |
|---|---|---|
| | NP1 | NP2 |
| Direct cost | 18.00 | 42.00 |
| Production overhead | 3.60 | 8.40 |
| Marketing and administration | 5.40 | 12.60 |
| 30% mark-up | 8.10 | 18.90 |
| Selling price | 35.10 | 81.90 |

### Sales Director's response:

Cynthia says that the spreadsheet prices are not competitive.

She knows that the business will suffer if she cannot refresh the product range with new products at attractive prices.

She has compared each of the two products (NP1 and NP2) with competitors' products and has estimated the sales potential at three price levels.

| Price levels and estimated annual volumes | NP1 | | NP2 | |
|---|---|---|---|---|
| | £ each | Volume | £ each | Volume |
| To undercut competition | 21.00 | 250 | 52.00 | 600 |
| Market price | 28.00 | 150 | 60.00 | 400 |
| Spreadsheet price | 35.10 | 50 | 81.90 | 150 |

Cynthia asks you to calculate which prices would be most profitable.

(a) **For each product calculate the marginal cost per unit and the annual contribution that would be earned at each of the two prices that Cynthia has considered.**

| Calculation of contribution | NP1 £ | NP2 £ |
|---|---|---|
| Marginal cost per unit (to the nearest penny) | | |

| Annual contribution | £ | £ |
|---|---|---|
| To undercut the competition | | |
| Market price | | |
| Spreadsheet price | | |

(8 marks)

(b) **Select the price that would give the highest contribution to profit for each of the two products.**

| Product | Best price |
|---|---|
| NP1 | ▼ |
| NP2 | ▼ |

**Picklist:**

Market price
Spreadsheet price
To undercut the competition

(2 marks)

(c) **Discuss the possible impact of Louise Harding's proposed policy on the business.**

**(5 marks)**

## Task 5 (20 marks)

Louise Harding, the Finance Director, is preparing a presentation for the Board of Directors. She has asked you to complete a comparative 'score card' of key financial ratios which she will use as part of her presentation.

Relevant data has been extracted from the last two years' accounts. These extracts do not include the results of Merville Ltd.

| Extracts from accounts of SL Products Ltd | Year ended 31 December 20X1 £000 | Year ended 31 December 20X2 £000 |
|---|---|---|
| Sales revenue | 20,000 | 20,900 |
| Cost of sales | 14,322 | 15,144 |
| Profit from operations | 1,265 | 470 |
| **Assets** | | |
| Non-current assets | 4,330 | 4,234 |
| Inventories | 3,614 | 3,908 |
| Trade receivables | 2,976 | 3,032 |
| Cash and equivalents | 8 | 6 |
| **Total** | **10,928** | **11,180** |

| Extracts from accounts of SL Products Ltd | Year ended 31 December 20X1 £000 | Year ended 31 December 20X2 £000 |
|---|---|---|
| **Equity and Liabilities** | | |
| Equity | 6,025 | 5,550 |
| Non-current liabilities | 1,200 | 1,400 |
| Trade payables | 3,360 | 3,730 |
| Bank overdraft | 124 | 260 |
| Tax liabilities | 219 | 240 |
| **Total** | **10,928** | **11,180** |

**(a)  Complete the scorecard by calculating the missing ratios.**

| SL Products Ltd Scorecard | Year ended 31 Dec 20X1 | Year ended 31 Dec 20X2 |
|---|---|---|
| **Profitability and gearing (correct to 1 dp):** | | |
| Gross profit % | 28.4% | ☐% |
| Operating profit % | 6.3% | 2.2% |
| Return on capital employed | 17.5% | ☐% |
| Gearing | 16.6% | 20.1% |
| **Liquidity ratios (correct to 1 dp):** | | |
| Current ratio | 1.8:1 | ☐:1 |
| Acid test/quick ratio | 0.8:1 | ☐:1 |
| **Working capital days (correct to nearest day):** | | |
| Inventory holding period | 92 days | 94 days |
| Trade receivables collection period | 54 days | 53 days |
| Trade payables payment period | 86 days | 90 days |
| Working capital cycle | 60 days | ☐ days |

**(10 marks)**

**(b)** Select the **ONE** correct observation about each aspect of business performance below.

**Profitability**

| | ✓ |
|---|---|
| This has been a year of steady, if unspectacular, progress. Although profitability has dipped, the return on capital employed has been kept under control. | |
| The profitability ratios give cause for concern. The small increase in sales revenue has not improved the gross profit percentage. Operating expenses have increased, reducing operating profit and return on capital employed. | |
| The ratios give mixed messages. Some have improved and some have deteriorated. Further investigation is required. | |

**(2 marks)**

**Gearing**

| | ✓ |
|---|---|
| The increased gearing ratio is entirely due to the increase in non-current liabilities. | |
| It is likely that the interest cover ratio has increased. | |
| The increased gearing ratio shows that the company has become more risky. | |

**(2 marks)**

**Liquidity**

| | ✓ |
|---|---|
| Both ratios have deteriorated which indicates that the company is less solvent. | |
| Both ratios remain too high, indicating that working capital is not being used effectively. | |
| Some liquidity ratios have improved and some have deteriorated. Further investigation is required to understand whether liquidity is improving. | |

**(2 marks)**

## Working capital

| | ✓ |
|---|---|
| The working capital cycle has worsened. The inventory holding period has improved but the other ratios indicate a lack of financial control. | |
| There is a welcome improvement in the working capital cycle, mainly due to the change in the payment period for payables. | |
| The working capital cycle is worse than a year ago because of the increased cost of sales. | |

**(2 marks)**

## Overall performance

| | ✓ |
|---|---|
| Profitability has declined in 20X2, mainly due to competitive pressures. However, the gearing and liquidity measures show an improving financial position. | |
| 20X2 has been a bad year. Profitability has declined and finances are coming under pressure. | |
| Steady progress has been made in 20X2. The ratios show that the company is being better managed. | |

**(2 marks)**

## Task 6 (15 marks)

You have been asked to carry out a review of SL Products Ltd's sales order processing procedure and make recommendations for improvement.

You have interviewed the Sales Director (Cynthia Moss), Credit controller (Ray Massey) and Accounts Receivable Clerk (Matthew Tunnock). Your findings are below.

## Catalogue

The 85-page illustrated catalogue is updated and posted to customers in the spring and autumn of each year. The print run is 5,000 copies. An online version is put on the company's website.

Orders can be placed by post, telephone or online if the customer has been granted credit terms. Otherwise, orders will only be accepted by post and must be paid for in advance by cheque (in British pounds). These cheques are cleared before despatch is allowed.

Accounts that are dormant for 18 months are closed. These customers are removed from the catalogue distribution list.

## Customer base

80% of sales are made to just 20% of the credit customers.

Most of these sales are repeat orders for some long-established items in the catalogue. 95% of sales, by value, are to credit account customers.

There are 4,210 customers with credit accounts: 4,000 in the UK; 150 in European Union countries and 60 elsewhere around the world. Over the last year, 129 new customers have been granted credit accounts. 608 inactive accounts have been closed.

Sales to customers outside the UK have declined over the last five years and now make up only 7% of total sales.

## Credit accounts

Account application forms are sent to new customers by Matthew Tunnock. Trade and bank references are required. When the forms and references are returned, Matthew checks them and drafts a confirmation letter which Ray Massey authorises.

Matthew sends the confirmation letter, a copy of the company's terms of trade and a catalogue to the new credit customer. There is no formal credit limit at this stage. Credit limits are placed on regular late payers.

Most customers settle their accounts within the agreed periods or very soon after. There are very few bad debts.

You are required to identify **four** features of these procedures: one strength, one weakness, one threat and one opportunity. Do not use the same feature more than once.

**(a)** Identify **ONE** strength in these procedures. Explain how the business benefits from this.

**(3 marks)**

**(b)** Identify **ONE** weakness in these procedures. Explain how this damages the business and suggest a remedy.

**(4 marks)**

**(c)** Identify an opportunity to improve the procedures. Explain how the procedure should be changed and how the business could benefit.

**(4 marks)**

**(d)** Identify ONE threat to the effectiveness of these procedures. Explain how this could damage the business and suggest an action that would reduce the risk.

**(4 marks)**

# AAT AQ2016 PRACTICE ASSESSMENT 1 LEVEL 4 SYNOPTIC ASSESSMENT

# ANSWERS

# Level 4 Synoptic Assessment
## AAT practice assessment 1

## Task 1 (20 marks)

**(a)** **Which of your principles is threatened by this request?**

| Confidentiality |
|---|

**How should you respond?**

| Base your analysis entirely on the published results |
|---|

**(4 marks)**

**(b)** Revaluation of premises

| Do not include |
|---|

Bonus issue of shares in SL Products Ltd

| Do not include |
|---|

Payment of dividend on ordinary shares

| Include in cash flow |
|---|

Write off obsolete inventory

| Do not include |
|---|

**(8 marks)**

**(c)** **Show whether each of the following errors and discrepancies would be detected by reconciling the accounts payable ledger to its control account by selecting your answers from the picklist.**

| Errors and discrepancies | Answer |
|---|---|
| A supplier has been paid for an invoice twice | Would not be detected |
| A supplier invoice has been posted to the wrong supplier account | Would not be detected |
| A cheque payment has been debited to the accounts receivable control account | Would be detected |
| VAT on some purchases has been omitted from the VAT return | Would not be detected |
| A purchase invoice has been debited to the account of a supplier | Would be detected |

**(d)** **What sort of access should Liz have to the accounts payable control account?**

| Read only access |
|---|

Liz only needs to view the data, so she does not need to change any data and therefore does not need 'full access, including data entry'. However, she needs read access so that she can ensure the accounts payable ledger agrees to its control account. Therefore, 'read only access' is appropriate for her role.

**(1 mark)**

**(e)** **Which of the following describes this suggestion?**

|  | ✓ |
|---|---|
| Acceptable commercial practice | |
| Unethical 'window dressing' | ✓ |
| Fraud | |
| Breach of the control environment | |

**(2 marks)**

## Task 2 (15 marks)

**(a)** **Examine the planning assumptions and calculations in the proposed budget and identify any weaknesses.**

The draft budget is based on the assumption of 10% growth in sales volume. No justification is offered for this round figure assumption. I suggest that we need to review recent trends in Merville Ltd's products, look at the potential for the anticipated new products and estimate the likely additional business generated from our own customers. With only 50 current products, this should not be difficult.

The assumption that sales revenue will only grow relative to sales volume is probably pessimistic. Although we are told prices can never be raised, new products should command a healthy margin when launched, particularly as they are patent protected.

All costs have been increased by 12.5% in the draft budget (2.5% for inflation and 10% for growth). There is no reason why fixed costs should increase by more than an appropriate rate for inflation. Each line of costs needs to be considered carefully according to its cost type (variable, fixed, etc) and its own cost pressures.

In particular, agreement is required about the management bonus. This has been accrued at £21,000 for 20X2 and, in effect, budgeted at £23,625 for 20X3. This has not yet been approved.

**(5 marks)**

**(b)** **Explain how costs and profitability should be managed in an organisation that manufactures multiple products.**

In a multi-product manufacturing organisation it is essential that costs and profitability are reviewed by product. Therefore, a costing system needs to be in place.

A standard costing system has particular advantages in that it is based on calculations of what the costs should be, called standard costs. This is useful for control as variances from these standards can be reported and investigated.

The standard cost of each product can be compared with its selling price to identify profitability.

Standard costs can be calculated for planned new products to inform price setting.

**(5 marks)**

**(c)** **Give your opinion, with reasons, on how well the budget would motivate managers to create sustainable, profitable growth.**

Budgetary control can be a powerful tool to encourage managers and staff to create sustainable, profitable growth. To do this, budgets need to be stretching but achievable.

The proposed Merville Ltd budget has been prepared by its own directors who have a vested interest, in the form of the management bonus, in ensuring that it is easy to achieve. They have not provided sufficient supporting data to enable us to verify that the sales volume and pricing assumptions are stretching.

Increasing all costs, fixed and variable, by 12.5% cannot be justified and creates significant budgetary slack.

I do not believe that this draft budget would motivate Merville Ltd to create sustainable, profitable growth.

**(5 marks)**

## Task 3 (15 marks)

**Complete your review as follows, using the provided answer spaces below:**

- **Identify five systemic weaknesses in the company's internal controls for handling purchases on credit.**

- **Explain how each weakness that you have identified could create a problem for the company.**

**Note.** There are more suggested answers shown below than are required to be given in the task. Awarded 1 mark for identification of the weakness and 2 (with a maximum of 3) for the explanation.

| No. | Weakness | Potential problem |
|-----|----------|-------------------|
| 1 | The purchasing manager appears to have very little involvement in day to day purchasing, apart from negotiating terms with new suppliers. | Failures in the system and system abuses could go unnoticed. |
| 2 | No apparent security for order stationery. | Potential for anyone to commit fraud by making purchases for their own use in the company's name. |
| 3 | Budget holders and the warehouse manager can raise orders and sign that the goods or services have been received. | There is a potential for fraud as there does not appear to be any check that these purchases are necessary, or even for business use. |
| 4 | The procedures do not include any mention of checking that goods and services of the correct standard have been received. | If this is not happening the company could be paying for unsatisfactory supplies. |
| 5 | There is no cash limit to purchase orders provided that they are within the approved budget. | Without a second signature on large purchases, there is scope for errors, poor judgement or fraud to be very costly. |
| 6 | Orders can be placed without agreeing a price. | The company is in a weak position to negotiate price after the goods or service have been received. |

| No. | Weakness | Potential problem |
|---|---|---|
| 7 | Lack of authorisation of new accounts. | There should be a policy for choosing new suppliers. Potential for fraud through collusion with suppliers. |
| 8 | The terms agreed by Tony Clark are not countersigned. | Potential for fraud through collusion with suppliers. |
| 9 | Only one signature is required on purchase orders. | Potential for fraud through collusion with suppliers. |
| 10 | Liz Hall checks, clears and arranges payment of invoices. | Potential for fraud through collusion with suppliers. |
| 11 | Tony Clark and Liz Hall control all aspects of purchase accounting. | Potential for fraud through collusion. |

**(15 marks)**

## Task 4 (15 marks)

(a) **For each product calculate the marginal cost per unit and the annual contribution that would be earned at each of the two prices that Cynthia has considered.**

| Calculation of contribution | NP1 £ | NP2 £ |
|---|---|---|
| Marginal cost per unit (to the nearest penny) | 20.70 | 48.30 |

**Working:** direct cost + (15% × direct cost)

| Annual contribution | £ | £ |
|---|---|---|
| To undercut the competition | 75 | 2,220 |
| Market price | 1,095 | 4,680 |
| Spreadsheet price | 720 | 5,040 |

**(8 marks)**

237

**(b)** **Select the price that would give the highest contribution to profit for each of the two products**

| Product | Best price |
|---------|------------|
| NP1 | Market price |
| NP2 | Spreadsheet price |

**(2 marks)**

**(c)** **Discuss the possible impact of Louise Harding's proposed policy on the business.**

In theory, any price that is higher than marginal cost will make a contribution and therefore increase profits. The policy generates prices which are greater than total unit cost, including an apportionment of fixed costs. Therefore they should be profitable at any volume of sale.

**Despite being profitable, the new policy could be damaging to the business.**

The pricing policy does not allow the Sales Director to respond to market conditions and find the combination of profit and volume that will optimise contribution.

SLP is in a price competitive business. If new products are not priced competitively they will only sell in small volumes. As ageing products decline they must be replaced by innovative new ones.

The business will go into decline if the product range is not refreshed.

**(5 marks)**

## Task 5 (20 marks)

**(a)** **Complete the scorecard by calculating the missing ratios.**

| SL Products Ltd Scorecard | Year ended 31 Dec 20X1 | Year ended 31 Dec 20X2 |
|---------------------------|------------------------|------------------------|
| **Profitability and gearing (correct to 1 dp):** | | |
| Gross profit % | 28.4% | 27.5 % |
| Operating profit % | 6.3% | 2.2% |
| Return on capital employed | 17.5% | 6.8 % |
| Gearing | 16.6% | 20.1% |

| SL Products Ltd Scorecard | Year ended 31 Dec 20X1 | Year ended 31 Dec 20X2 |
|---|---|---|
| **Liquidity ratios (correct to 1 dp):** | | |
| Current ratio | 1.8:1 | 1.6 :1 |
| Acid test/quick ratio | 0.8:1 | 0.7 :1 |
| **Working capital days (correct to nearest day):** | | |
| Inventory holding period | 92 days | 94 days |
| Trade receivables collection period | 54 days | 53 days |
| Trade payables payment period | 86 days | 90 days |
| Working capital cycle | 60 days | 57 days |

**(10 marks)**

**(b)** **Select the ONE correct observation about each aspect of business performance below.**

**Profitability**

| | ✓ |
|---|---|
| This has been a year of steady, if unspectacular, progress. Although profitability has dipped, the return on capital employed has been kept under control. | |
| The profitability ratios give cause for concern. The small increase in sales revenue has not improved the gross profit percentage. Operating expenses have increased, reducing operating profit and return on capital employed. | ✓ |
| The ratios give mixed messages. Some have improved and some have deteriorated. Further investigation is required. | |

**(2 marks)**

## Gearing

| | ✓ |
|---|---|
| The increased gearing ratio is entirely due to the increase in non-current liabilities. | |
| It is likely that the interest cover ratio has increased. | |
| The increased gearing ratio shows that the company has become more risky. | ✓ |

**(2 marks)**

## Liquidity

| | ✓ |
|---|---|
| Both ratios have deteriorated which indicates that the company is less solvent. | ✓ |
| Both ratios remain too high, indicating that working capital is not being used effectively. | |
| Some liquidity ratios have improved and some have deteriorated. Further investigation is required to understand whether liquidity is improving. | |

**(2 marks)**

## Working capital

| | ✓ |
|---|---|
| The working capital cycle has worsened. The inventory holding period has improved but the other ratios indicate a lack of financial control. | |
| There is a welcome improvement in the working capital cycle, mainly due to the change in the payment period for payables. | ✓ |
| The working capital cycle is worse than a year ago because of the increased cost of sales. | |

**(2 marks)**

**Overall performance**

|  | ✓ |
|---|---|
| Profitability has declined in 20X2, mainly due to competitive pressures. However, the gearing and liquidity measures show an improving financial position. | |
| 20X2 has been a bad year. Profitability has declined and finances are coming under pressure. | ✓ |
| Steady progress has been made in 20X2. The ratios show that the company is being better managed. | |

**(2 marks)**

## Task 6 (15 marks)

**(a)** **Identify ONE strength in these procedures. Explain how the business benefits from this.**

Effective credit control is in place. New applicants for accounts are credit checked and there is routine credit control. This minimises bad debts and assists cash flow.

**(3 marks)**

**(b)** **Identify ONE weakness in these procedures. Explain how this damages the business and suggest a remedy.**

It is not easy for new customers to place orders, particularly from overseas. The requirement to apply for credit terms or to send a cheque through the post is an obstacle to trade and is probably sending potential customers elsewhere. Only 5% of sales are made against cleared cheques.

The account opening procedure needs to be performed electronically. Customers should be able to apply online for a small initial credit limit which can be immediately checked with a credit reference agency. Alternatively, a facility to pay online by credit or debit card when placing an order would be attractive to small businesses and those with a poor credit record.

**(4 marks)**

(c) **Identify an opportunity to improve the procedures. Explain how the procedure should be changed and how the business could benefit.**

There appears to be an opportunity to improve relations with customers. Printed catalogues are expensive to produce and distribute and not as effective as targeted electronic communications. Customers could be sent daily electronic mail shots tailored to their own buying records and browsing history. The catalogue could be updated daily.

This could save money and should boost sales.

**(4 marks)**

(d) **Identify ONE threat to the effectiveness of these procedures. Explain how this could damage the business and suggest an action that would reduce the risk.**

We operate in a competitive environment. 80% of our sales are made to just 840, or so, customers and consist mainly of repeat orders for established products. We are vulnerable if our competitors offer new or cheaper products to these customers.

We must protect this business by ensuring that we develop or buy the best available products at competitive prices.

**(4 marks)**

BPP
LEARNING MEDIA

# AAT AQ2016 PRACTICE ASSESSMENT 2 LEVEL 4 SYNOPTIC ASSESSMENT

*You are advised to attempt the sample assessment online from the AAT website. This will ensure you are prepared for how the assessment will be presented on the AAT's system when you attempt the real assessment. Please access the assessment using the address below:*

https://www.aat.org.uk/training/study-support/search

The AAT may call the assessments on their website, under study support resources, either a 'practice assessment' or 'sample assessment'.

# Scenario Overview
# LEVEL 4 SYNOPTIC ASSESSMENT

## Holly's Hot Tubs Ltd

**For assessments 1 September 2021**

BPP Practice Assessment 3 will help you prepare for your live assessment by using the Holly's Hot Tubs Ltd scenario.

# Scenario

*Version correct as at 6 May 2021, please check online at www.aat.org.uk to ensure you have the latest version*

## HOLLY'S HOT TUBS LTD

### Company background

Holly's Hot Tubs Ltd commenced trading two years ago when Holly Turner saw an increasing demand from houseowners for home lifestyle products.

Holly has created and developed several successful businesses over the previous 20 years, all based on the same strategy:

- find a growing market;
- advertise extensively;
- invest in high quality experienced staff; and
- keep fixed overheads as low as possible to minimise operational risk.

This model has been applied to Holly's Hot Tubs Ltd. To provide control and direction, a five-year plan was established at the incorporation of the business. The plan is updated at the end of each year based upon operational performance in the previous 12 months and an analysis of future market expectations.

The exit strategy is to develop Holly's Hot Tubs Ltd over a five-year period to a point where it will be an attractive investment opportunity for either a competitor or someone looking to enter the market. Holly looks to sell her businesses at a multiple of two times the average revenue over the five-year period.

### Performance to date

For the first year the business enjoyed a successful start with sales being far higher than originally predicted. However, the start of the second year's trading was much more challenging. Sales reduced and costs increased significantly, putting a strain on both profitability and cashflow.

To try and improve the sales performance the business took the decision to make two changes:

- selling prices would be reduced by 10% with a price match guarantee against any equivalent product and

- payment terms for customers would be increased.

The original terms required customers to pay in full for a hot tub when the order was placed, however this was changed to allow customers to pay just 20% at the time of the order with the balance due within seven days of delivery. On average, the lead time from the customer placing the order to delivery is eight weeks.

The products sold by the business are imported from overseas and suppliers require payment from Holly's Hot Tubs Ltd within seven days of delivery. By extending the customer payment period, the working capital cycle of the business increased significantly and so the increase in sales following the pricing reduction put a strain on the cashflow of the business.

Until recently, the business had rented a showroom and offices in a semi-rural location approximately 20 miles from Leeds in West Yorkshire. The property was owned by a friend of Holly and the agreement was a rolling 12-month contract for a nominal rent, on the basis that the premises was refurbished and maintained throughout the period of occupation.

After a period of time Holly identified that a showroom was not particularly important to customers. Almost all customers would look at products on the company's website, compare prices and models against competitors, and make their purchase remotely. As a result, the rental of the premises was terminated at the end of the second year of trading with all staff moving to home-based working, using internet-based technology for meetings.

In addition to the sales of hot tubs, the business also has two other associated income streams that have been very profitable.

### Servicing

For a customer to keep their hot tub guarantee valid, it is a requirement that the hot tub is serviced on an annual basis. The internal mechanics of hot tubs are basic and therefore servicing is relatively straightforward and does not need highly skilled staff. Additional income can also be earned through any repairs that may need to be undertaken on items not covered by the warranty.

To try and simplify this part of the business, Holly decided that the servicing would be sub-contracted to other firms, on a fixed fee basis.

### Consumables

All hot tubs require chemicals to be added on a regular basis to maintain water quality and water filters need to be replaced frequently to maintain hot tub performance. To maximise sales, Holly's Hot Tubs Ltd combine the chemicals and filters into a single package and sell them through the website. Excellent margins are achieved on these sales.

### Operational issues

Despite the overall strong start to the business from a sales perspective, there have been several operational issues that have started to have an impact on the company's profitability.

### Delivery

Delivery and installation of the hot tubs are made by specialist delivery firms. Before a firm can deliver for Holly's Hot Tubs Ltd their staff must attend a course on

how to install the products. Due to high staff turnover levels in these businesses, there have been several complaints by customers about both the professionalism and technical competence of the staff making deliveries.

### Servicing

The decision to sub-contract out the servicing has also led to quality issues for the business. There have been numerous complaints from customers where either the sub-contractor failed to turn up for the service or customers have felt pressurised into changing parts unnecessarily.

### Social media

Both the delivery and servicing issues have resulted in negative feedback being left on a trade review site. Holly's Hot Tubs Ltd has always prided itself on excellent customer feedback and has links from its website to the trade review organisation.

### Staff

The closing of the office and the subsequent home-based roles for staff has resulted in a decline in staff morale. The weekly staff meetings that took place at the office no longer happen and staff feel that there is a lack of leadership and direction within the business.

### Cashflow

The reduction in selling prices, together with the changed payment terms, has put a significant strain on the finances of the business. In order to provide sufficient working capital for the business a substantial loan has been taken out with a floating charge over the assets of the business.

## Recent developments

As a result of Holly's Hot Tubs Ltd reducing prices, one of its main competitors has undertaken a national marketing campaign offering three years' free servicing with any new hot tub and extending the manufacturer's guarantee by another two years. The campaign appears to have been successful as there has been a noticeable reduction in the level of sales made by the business since the competitor's actions.

Last month an offer was made for the business by this competitor who was willing to pay two times the average profits made to date. Although Holly felt it was a good offer for the business, she had concerns as to whether the existing staff would retain their jobs moving forward and so the offer was rejected.

Over the last few months, the business has experienced supply issues. There has been a rise by over 90% in the cost of container transports. These increases have also been affected by movements in exchange rates. All purchases are made in US dollars and the pound has significantly weakened against the dollar causing costs to increase.

To further develop the business, Holly decided that there was an opportunity to expand the product offering by also selling saunas and steam rooms. Holly felt that these new products complemented hot tubs and that the customer base for each would be similar.

In the first two years, Holly's Hot Tubs Ltd only sold to customers in the UK but it was decided that there was no reason why sales could not be made to other countries. As a starting point in widening the sales reach of the business, it was agreed to extend sales to customers based in the Republic of Ireland.

### Five-year plan extract – sales analysis

| Year | Actual 1 | Actual 2 | Plan 3 | Plan 4 | Plan 5 |
|---|---|---|---|---|---|
| **Sales (units)** | | | | | |
| | | | | | |
| Hot tubs | 154 | 198 | 250 | 300 | 350 |
| Saunas | | | 20 | 50 | 100 |
| Steam rooms | | | 10 | 40 | 80 |
| Servicing | | 57 | 99 | 140 | 195 |
| Consumables | 221 | 299 | 500 | 600 | 700 |

## Staff

Some of Holly's Hot Tubs Ltd's key personnel are listed below:

| | |
|---|---|
| Chairman & Chief Executive | Holly Turner |
| Sales Director | Rik Alden |
| Finance Director | Malik Kain |
| Office Manager | Elisa Kendrick |
| Sales Manager | Kristopher Ward |
| Sales Executive | Jason Schroder |
| Operations Manager | Rigby Holmes |
| Purchasing Manager | Binny Hameer |
| Accounts Payable Manager | Danielle Collinson |

| | | |
|---|---|---|
| General Accounts Clerk | Maisie Fox | |
| Payroll Manager | Niels Erasmus | |

## Holly's Hot Tubs Ltd financial statements

**Holly's Hot Tubs Ltd – Statement of profit or loss for the year ended 31 October**

| | 31/10/X2 £ | 31/10/X1 £ |
|---|---|---|
| **Revenue** | 1,684,720 | 1,321,155 |
| Cost of sales | (993,985) | (660,577) |
| **Gross profit** | 690,735 | 660,578 |
| Operating expenses | (657,041) | (449,193) |
| **Profit from operations** | 33,694 | 211,385 |
| Finance costs | (6,260) | (350) |
| **Profit before tax** | 27,434 | 211,035 |
| Tax | (5,213) | (40,097) |
| **Profit for the period from continuing operations** | 22,221 | 170,938 |

**Holly Hot Tubs Ltd – Statement of financial position as at 31 October**

| | 31/10/X2 £ | 31/10/X1 £ |
|---|---|---|
| **ASSETS** | | |
| **Non-current assets** | | |
| Property, plant and equipment | 32,004 | 46,256 |
| | 32,004 | 46,256 |
| **Current assets** | | |
| Inventories | 178,425 | 178,889 |

| | 31/10/X2 | 31/10/X1 |
|---|---|---|
| | £ | £ |
| Trade receivables | 247,600 | 0 |
| Cash and cash equivalents | 55,089 | 130,168 |
| | 481,114 | 309,057 |
| **Total assets** | 513,118 | 355,313 |
| **EQUITY AND LIABILITIES** | | |
| **Equity** | | |
| Ordinary share capital (£1 shares) | 100 | 100 |
| Retained earnings | 193,159 | 170,938 |
| **Total equity** | 193,259 | 171,038 |
| **Non-current liabilities** | | |
| Bank loan | 148,000 | 10,000 |
| | 148,000 | 10,000 |
| **Current liabilities** | | |
| Trade payables | 166,646 | 134,178 |
| Tax liabilities | 5,213 | 40,097 |
| | 171,859 | 174,275 |
| **Total liabilities** | 319,859 | 184,275 |
| **Total equity and liabilities** | 513,118 | 355,313 |

# Synoptic assessment
# Analysis of scenario: Holly's Hot Tubs Ltd

For assessments starting September 2021, AAT have issued a new live pre-release scenario, Holly's Hot Tubs Ltd (www.aat.org.uk/training/study-support/search).

It is essential that you have reviewed this prior to sitting your assessment. The synoptic assessment is designed to test your knowledge and application skills, and pull them together to demonstrate strong problem solving techniques.

Here is a summary of some of the key points from the pre-release information. This is not an exhaustive analysis, and there are areas which would benefit from further review and investigation.

You will be given narratives as well as financial information during the assessment in addition to the pre-release information. This is not available before the assessment, so be prepared to use this additional resource and adapt your answers accordingly.

If possible, investigate the financial statements of similar companies that sell and install hot tubs and related components and ratios. You will then be able to comment on whether the ratios and metrics for Holly's Hot Tubs Ltd are in line with expectations.

A word on ratios: Ratios should be commented on, not just calculated and stated. If the information is available, compare it to previous years or to competitors' results. Consider what the ratio is telling you. If you are asked to discuss or explain or conclude information from a ratio, ensure you have given a justification for the movement (provided it is sensible and supported by facts, you will gain credit).

## Key information provided

Please note that this information is not exhaustive and will give you a start on your pre-assessment analysis of the scenario.

### Overall analysis of the pre-release material

One way of analysing a company is to prepare a SWOT analysis.

You may be asked to use this information to provide a report to Holly Turner and the other directors for consideration when deciding whether the offer received from the competitor is reasonable.

Ensure that you are familiar with producing a variety of reports, including a balanced scorecard based on the SWOT analysis. You may also be asked to comment about some of the strengths, weaknesses, opportunities and threats identified.

The following is not exhaustive and you are encouraged to build on this SWOT analysis to become familiar with the scenario and potential areas of risk.

| Strengths | Weaknesses |
|---|---|
| • Experienced senior management team (no recent additions or movements noted in the scenario) with a clear plan for how they want the business to develop<br><br>• Evidence of demand in the market for the products sold due to success of competitor.<br><br>• Good offer made to buy Holly's Hot Tubs Ltd indicates that competitor sees value in the business. | • Cash flow and working capital management problems. The company appears to be running out of cash quickly.<br><br>• Low morale of staff due to closure of showroom could lead to high staff turnover.<br><br>• Reputational issues caused by issues around delivery and installation and poor performance of sub-contractors performing servicing.<br><br>• Negative reviews on social media likely to put off future customers.<br><br>• Large loan has been used for working capital purposes. Company has increased liabilities without making investment in assets which is not sustainable.<br><br>• Supply issues causing concerns about continuity of supply. |

| Strengths | Weaknesses |
|---|---|
|  | • Declining financial performance: <br><br>   – Gross profit margin declined from 50% in X1 to 41% in X2 <br><br>   – Operating profit margin declined from 16% in X1 to 2% in X2 <br><br>   – Return on capital employed declined from 117% in X1 to 14% in X2 |

| Opportunities | Threats |
|---|---|
| • Sale of consumables forecast to increase significantly and margins achieved on these are excellent <br><br> • Diversification into saunas and steam rooms allow opportunity for new revenue streams. <br><br> • Overseas customers also offer opportunity for new revenue streams. <br><br> • Forecast sales units are good. Could be profitable and improve cash flows if margins are good. <br><br> • Large trade receivable of £247,600. Collecting this would significantly improve cash position. <br><br> • Opportunity to better manage costs by managing foreign exchange rates. | • Business is running out of cash. Bank loan appears to be almost fully utilised and repayment will be a burden. <br><br> • Loan gives bank floating charge over the company's assets. Going concern risk if cash position means loan repayments can't be made. <br><br> • Competition in the market is strong which forces down prices and makes it more difficult to be the supplier of choice for customers. <br><br> • Risk that margins continue to be squeezed in attempt to attract customers. |

**Further steps**

• Calculate ratios on the pre-release information as far as the information allows.

• Ensure you understand the benefits and issues with using certain ratios and can justify why you have used those particular ratios and not others.

• Review the financial statements of real-life companies who sell and install hot tubs and related products and services, as this will broaden your knowledge and potentially highlight more issues which businesses in this sector can face, for example, www.jacuzzi.co.uk

BPP LEARNING MEDIA

- AAT like to bring current issues in their Level 4 *Professional Diploma of Accounting Synoptic* assessment, so it is advisable to read financial papers, online news or look up financial statements on Companies House website. Some of these useful links will give you some material to start with.

- Please note that this list is not exhaustive and there may be elements for further discussion you have spotted or you think are relevant to the scenario.

## Useful links

Sales surge in 2020 provides welcome boost for wet leisure industry (2021). Available online at https://www.bishta.co.uk/category/bishta-blog/ [Accessed 6 May 2021]

Hot tub sales rise by 1,000% (2020). Available online at https://www.thisismoney.co.uk/money/news/article-8414201/Hot-tub-sales-rise-1-000-Britons-enjoy-hot-weather.html [Accessed 6 May 2021]

Hot tub damage: complaints soar (2020). Available online at https://www.thisismoney.co.uk/money/news/article-8744543/Hot-tub-damage-Complaints-soar-sales-surged-lockdown.html [Accessed 6 May 2021]

How to manage negative reviews on social media (2019). Available online at: https://www.businessknowhow.com/internet/negativereviews.htm [Accessed 6 May 2021)

How to prioritise staff morale when you are working remotely (2020. Available online at https://www.roberthalf.co.uk/blog/human-resource-management/how-prioritise-team-morale-when-you-are-working-semi-remotely [Accessed 6 May 2021].

Three quarters of entrepreneurs stay on after selling business (2018). *Business Matters*. Available online at: www.bmmagazine.co.uk/in-business/three-quarters-of-entrepreneurs-stay-on-after-selling-business/ [Accessed 6 May 2021].

# BPP PRACTICE ASSESSMENT 3
# LEVEL 4 SYNOPTIC ASSESSMENT

**Time allowed: 3 hours**

**PRACTICE ASSESSMENT 3**

# Level 4 Synoptic Assessment
# BPP practice assessment 3

This practice assessment is based on the same scenario as AAT's live assessment, Holly's Hot Tubs Ltd for assessments from 1 September 2021. See pages 247–252 for the relevant pre-reading material, and the latest version can be obtained from www.aat.org.uk

## Task 1 (20 marks)

Malik Kain, the Finance Director, is responsible for preparing Holly's Hot Tubs Ltd's financial statements. He is preparing notes to explain to the other directors the basis on which the financial statements are prepared.

**(a)** **Complete the following statement.**

The fundamental qualitative characteristics that underlie the preparation of useful general purpose financial statements are [＿＿＿＿＿＿＿▼] and [＿＿＿＿＿＿＿▼]. It is a requirement that the financial statements, unless stated otherwise, are prepared on a [＿＿＿＿＿＿＿▼] basis.

**Picklist:**

cash
faithful representation
material
going concern
relevance

**(3 marks)**

The other directors have asked Malik if the financial statements he has prepared for the year will satisfy the information needs of the company's key stakeholders. Malik has explained that stakeholders have different information needs.

**(b)** **Identify which of the following provides the MOST useful information to the key stakeholders identified below:**

| | |
|---|---|
| Potential new investors to the company | [＿＿＿＿＿＿＿▼] |
| Board of Directors | [＿＿＿＿＿＿＿▼] |
| HM Revenue & Customs | [＿＿＿＿＿＿＿▼] |

**Picklist:**

Balanced scorecard of the company
Corporation tax return for the period
Financial statements as filed with the Registrar of Companies
Statement of cash flows
Statement of financial position

**(3 marks)**

The finance department has a written internal control which requires a bank reconciliation to be prepared on a weekly basis. The bank reconciliation is performed in an Excel spreadsheet which is emailed to Malik for his review before any adjusting journal entries are posted.

**(c)** **Maisie Fox, the General Accounts Clerk, has asked you to help her to understand whether the following would be detected by preparing a bank reconciliation.**

| | |
|---|---|
| A payment was made to Tubs Supplies rather than Spa Supplies | ▼ |
| A cheque payment to Greenside & Co has not yet been banked by the supplier | ▼ |
| A transposition error was made when recording a receipt in the cash book | ▼ |
| A bank transfer was received by the bank but was omitted from the cash book | ▼ |

**Picklist:**

Would be detected
Would not be detected

**(4 marks)**

**(d)** **Which type of control is Malik performing in respect of the bank reconciliation?**

| | ✓ |
|---|---|
| A supervisory control | |
| A general IT control | |
| An authorisation control | |
| Segregation of duties | |

**(2 marks)**

Holly's Hot Tubs Ltd increased its standard payment terms for customers from 30 days in 20X1 to 45 days in 20X2 in order to boost sales. Holly's Hot Tubs does not have a credit control department and all members of the finance team are occasionally involved in credit control.

**(e) Ideally, the security settings for an employee working in a credit control department should permit them access to which of the following?**

| | ✓ |
|---|---|
| The accounts receivable ledger only | |
| The accounts receivable ledger and the cash book | |
| The accounts receivable ledger and the general ledger | |
| The accounts receivable ledger, the general ledger and the cash book | |

**(2 marks)**

Your duties at Holly's Hot Tubs Ltd include reconciling the accounts receivable control account to the individual accounts receivable ledger balances. You have become aware that an individual balance in respect of credit customer Mr Palmer was written off despite a cheque payment from that customer being received. You raised the issue with Malik who advised you that he will deal with this account. He has asked you not to tell any other members of the finance team about this and has said that your compliance will be remembered when performance-related pay rises are next awarded.

**(f) Answer the following questions.**

Which of your fundamental ethical principles is threatened by this request?

**Picklist:**

Confidentiality
Objectivity
Professional competence and due care
What action should you take?

**Picklist:**

You must comply with Malik's instruction and remain silent
You must speak with other members of the finance team
You must raise the issue with Holly Turner
You must resign

Which of the following would NOT be helpful in preventing and detecting fraud in the sales and receivables system?

| | ✓ |
|---|---|
| Reviewing new credit customer accounts for evidence that credit checks had been performed | |
| Ensuring that all orders are checked to current inventory levels before being accepted | |
| Comparing the amount of irrecoverable debts written off from one year to another | |
| Requiring that adjustments to standard selling process are authorised by an appropriate person | |

**(6 marks)**

## Task 2 (15 marks)

Holly Turner has been reviewing the past budgets of Holly's Hot Tubs Ltd in preparation for a meeting on the future strategy of the company following the purchase offer from the competitor. She has noticed that there are invariably adverse variances in the sale of hot tubs revenue budget and favourable variances in the sale of consumables revenue budget.

The finance team set the individual budgets for the sale of the hot tubs. Rik Alden, the Sales Director, inputs into the budgets for the sale of consumables.

(a) **Suggest why the identified variances occur in the budgeting process for the hot tubs and consumables. In your answer, suggest how the situation could be improved.**

BPP
LEARNING MEDIA

**(7 marks)**

In order to improve sales performance, Holly Hunter is considering the introduction of performance related pay for the sales team

**(b)** **Explain the elements that must be in place in order for performance related pay to be a motivating factor for the sales team and explain the ethical and goal congruence issues that may arise as a result of the proposed performance related pay.**

(8 marks)

## Task 3 (15 marks)

The directors of Holly's Hot Tubs Ltd are concerned about the increased costs of supply. The company has internal controls in place in respect of its purchases and payables cycle, however the directors believe they may have uncovered a fraud being perpetrated by Binny Hameer, the Purchasing Manager. You have been provided with the following information relating to the purchases and payables cycle and the perceived fraud.

The company operates an accounting software package which includes a purchases and payments module. Binny Hameer, the Purchasing Manager, is responsible for making all purchases of goods for resale. Danielle Collinson, the Accounts Payable Manager, is responsible for managing the payments to suppliers, supported by Maisie Fox, the General Accounts Clerk.

Binny's responsibilities include:

- Establishing a list of approved suppliers. Binny has created the list based on contacts that he had from his previous roles

- Raising purchase orders. Purchase orders over £10,000 require additional authorisation from one of the directors

- Review and acceptance of goods received.

- Receipt of invoices from suppliers which are then passed to Maisie for processing.

Danielle's responsibilities include:

- Maintaining standing data, including putting new suppliers on the system, adding supplier bank accounts and supplier details to the purchase ledger.

- Making payments to suppliers by processing the BACS payments list prepared by Maisie on a weekly basis (the weekly payment run). No review of the list is undertaken and no payments to suppliers are made outside of this weekly window.

- Recording any discounts received from suppliers (the discounts are negotiated by Binny).

Maisie Fox's responsibilities include:

- Inputting the invoices agreed by Binny into the system
- Preparing the BACS payment list of all invoices due to be paid in the week

**(a)** **Identify FIVE internal control weaknesses in the company's purchasing and payables system.**

**(5 marks)**

**(b)** **Explain how each of the indentified weakneses could create opportunties for fraud and error to arise in the purchases and payables system of Holly's Hot Tubs Ltd.**

**(10 marks)**

| Weakness | Opportunity for fraud and error |
|---|---|
|  |  |
|  |  |
|  |  |
|  |  |
|  |  |

........................................................................

## Task 4 (15 marks)

A board meeting was recently held to discuss the proposed diversification into the sale of saunas and steam rooms. Malik has prepared the following forecast information for saunas and steam rooms for year 3.

The saunas and steam rooms are both sourced from different suppliers. The directors have identified a local supplier for the saunas which has an excellent reputation for quality and using sustainable wood in the products. The steam rooms are made from non-recycled plastic and would be sourced from a foreign supplier. The skill and time involved in installation is similar for both products.

The forecasts for products for the year ending 31 December 20X3 are below:

|  | Saunas | | Steam Rooms | |
|---|---|---|---|---|
| Sales units | 20 | | 10 | |
|  | £ | | £ | |
| Revenue | 47,200 | | 31,600 | |
| Purchase of goods for resale | 20,400 | | 16,800 | |
| Labour costs | 10,500 | | 5,800 | |
| Other cost of sales | 2,100 | | 1,300 | |
| Gross profit | 14,200 | 30% | 7,700 | 24% |

| | Saunas | | Steam Rooms | |
|---|---|---|---|---|
| Sales and distribution costs | 4,720 | | 3,160 | |
| Administration costs | 680 | | 410 | |
| Profit from operations | 8,800 | 19% | 4,130 | 13% |

Other information:

- The purchase of goods for resale are a variable cost as orders would only be placed with the supplier when a sale was made. A fixed-price supply contract would be entered into with supplier of saunas. The cost of purchase of steam rooms would be based in the foreign currency and the price may fluctuate during the year.

- The labour costs are variable. A labour rate increase is expected to be applied during the year but the amount of increase has not yet been determined.

- Sales and distribution costs are variable in proportion to the number of units sold.

- Other cost of sales and administration costs are fixed.

Due to uncertainty in the wet leisure market, Holly Turner is wondering whether it would be less risky to diversify into either the sale of saunas **OR** the sale of steam rooms in year 3 rather than diversifying into both. She considers that:

- If only the saunas OR Steam rooms were offered, it is expected that the sale of the single product would be higher. The increase would be the equivalent of 50% of the sales volume that was originally expected from the second product, for example if saunas were not offered as a product for sale, the sale of steam rooms would increase to 20, being the 10 forecast plus 50% of the forecast sauna sales.

- Other cost of sales would be a flat £2,000 regardless of which product was sold and administrative expenses would be a flat £500.

- The cost of purchase of saunas will fall by 5% per unit for all additional saunas between 21 and 25 units and by 10% per unit for all additional saunas over 26 units sold.

**(a)** **Assess the option of selling both saunas and steam rooms and the option to sell only the saunas in year 3. Your assessment should focus on the financial performance of the products.**

**(7 marks)**

**(b) Identify and explain any important non-financial information the directors should consider when assessing the options.**

**(8 marks)**

## Task 5 (20 marks)

Malik is preparing a presentation for the board of directors. He has asked you to complete a comparative 'score card' of key financial ratios which she will use as part of her presentation.

Relevant data has been extracted from the last two years' accounts.

| | 31/10/X2 £ | 31/10/X1 £ |
|---|---|---|
| **Revenue** | 1,684,720 | 1,321,155 |
| Cost of sales | (993,985) | (660,577) |
| **Gross profit** | 690,735 | 660,578 |
| Operating expenses | (657,041) | (449,193) |
| **Profit from operations** | 33,694 | 211,385 |
| Finance costs | (6,260) | (350) |
| **Profit before tax** | 27,434 | 211,035 |
| Tax | (5,213) | (40,097) |
| **Profit for the period from continuing operations** | 22,221 | 170,938 |

**Holly Hot Tubs Ltd – Statement of financial position as at 31 October**

| | 31/10/X2 £ | 31/10/X1 £ |
|---|---|---|
| **ASSETS** | | |
| **Non-current assets** | | |
| Property, plant and equipment | 32,004 | 46,256 |
| | 32,004 | 46,256 |

| | 31/10/X2 £ | 31/10/X1 £ |
|---|---|---|
| **Current assets** | | |
| Inventories | 178,425 | 178,889 |
| Trade receivables | 247,600 | 0 |
| Cash and cash equivalents | 55,089 | 130,168 |
| | 481,114 | 309,057 |
| **Total assets** | 513,118 | 355,313 |
| **EQUITY AND LIABILITIES** | | |
| **Equity** | | |
| Ordinary share capital (£1 shares) | 100 | 100 |
| Retained earnings | 193,159 | 170,938 |
| **Total equity** | 193,259 | 171,038 |
| **Non-current liabilities** | | |
| Bank loan | 148,000 | 10,000 |
| | 148,000 | 10,000 |
| **Current liabilities** | | |
| Trade payables | 166,646 | 134,178 |
| Tax liabilities | 5,213 | 40,097 |
| | 171,859 | 174,275 |
| **Total liabilities** | 319,859 | 184,275 |
| **Total equity and liabilities** | 513,118 | 355,313 |

**(a)** **Complete the scorecard by calculating the missing ratios for the year ended 31 October 20X2.**

| Holly's Hot Tubs Ltd Scorecard | Year ended 31 October 20X2 | Year ended 31 October 20X1 |
|---|---|---|
| **Profitability and working capital ratios** | | |
| Gross profit % | 41% | 50% |
| Operating profit % | ____% | 16% |
| Return on capital employed % | 10% | 117% |
| Gearing (calculated as debt/(debt + equity)) % | ____% | 6% |
| Current ratio | 2.8:1 | 1.8:1 |
| Receivables collection period | ____Days | 0 Days |
| Payables payment period (use cost of sales) | 61 Days | 74 Days |
| Inventory holding period | ____Days | 49 Days |
| Working capital cycle | ____Days | (25) Days |

**(5 marks)**

**(b)** **Select the ONE most appropriate observation about each aspect of business performance below.**

**Profitability**

| | ✓ |
|---|---|
| The gross profit has decreased due to a penalty paid for early termination of the rental of the head office. | |
| Operating profit has decreased due to the finance cost incurred on the loan. | |
| Gross profit has decreased due to the 10% reduction in selling prices. | |

**(2 marks)**

## Gearing

| | ✓ |
|---|---|
| The increased gearing ratio is due to the fall in cash and cash equivalents in 20X2 | |
| The increased gearing ratio is due to the bank loan taken out in 20X2 | |
| The increased gearing ratio is due to the additional interest costs incurred in 20X2 | |

**(2 marks)**

## Liquidity

| | ✓ |
|---|---|
| Liquidity has improved in 20X2 due to the existence of trade receivables | |
| An increased current ratio indicates that more cash is available to the company | |
| The faster payment of trade payables contributes to the decreased cash and cash equivalents balance | |

**(2 marks)**

## Working capital

| | ✓ |
|---|---|
| The lengthening inventory holding period indicates that the company is finding it easier to sell its products | |
| The decreasing trade payables payment period has a positive impact on working capital | |
| The increasing trade receivables collection period has a negative impact on working capital | |

**(2 marks)**

## Overall performance

| | ✓ |
|---|---|
| The financial statements show that the company paid a dividend in the year ended 31 October 20X1 | |
| The financial statements show that a loan was obtained for the purposes of working capital in the year ended 31 October 20X2 | |
| The financial statements show that the company is less risky at 31 October 20X2 than in the prior year | |

**(2 marks)**

.................................................................................................

## Task 6 (15 marks)

The directors of Holly's Hot Tubs Ltd have not undertaken a review of the internal controls in place at the company since its inception two years ago. They have been provided with the following information from Niels Erasmus, the Payroll Manager who was appointed in May 20X2, regarding staffing and payroll:

- The current payroll module was intended for companies with up to 20 employees. Holly's Hot Tubs Ltd currently has 24 full-time and 12 part-time employees.

- The current payroll module calculates statutory deductions for income tax and national insurance contributions. Any other deductions are manually calculated and input by Niels. There were instances of errors in the calculation of statutory and other deductions during the year.

- Niels is responsible for adding employees to the payroll module and for entering and amending the standing data. There is no additional check of any amendments.

- Employees are paid based on hours worked × hourly rate. The hours worked are assumed to be 35 hours for full-time employees and 16 hours for part-time employees unless Niels is advised otherwise by the employee's manager.

- Employees who work overtime at the weekend are paid at a rate of 1.5 times the normal hourly rate whereas overtime worked on a weekday is paid at the normal hourly rate. The employee's manager advises Niels whether overtime is worked at the weekend or on a weekday.

- Niels prepares a monthly listing of the payroll which he passes to Maisie Fox for payment. Maisie processes the payroll listing as provided by Niels.

273

(a) **Explain why it is appropriate for the directors to review the internal controls in respect of payroll.**

(6 marks)

(b) **Identify THREE control weaknesses and recommend a suitable improvement that should be made in respect of each of the weaknesses identified.**

(9 marks)

| Weakness | Suitable improvement |
|---|---|
|  |  |
|  |  |
|  |  |

# BPP PRACTICE ASSESSMENT 3
# LEVEL 4 SYNOPTIC ASSESSMENT

# ANSWERS

# Level 4 Synoptic Assessment
## BPP practice assessment 3: answers

## Task 1 (20 marks)

**(a)** The fundamental qualitative characteristics that underlie the preparation of useful general purpose financial statements are ☐ relevance ☐ and ☐ faithful representation ☐. It is a requirement that the financial statements, unless stated otherwise, are prepared on a ☐ going concern ☐ basis.

**(3 marks)**

**(b)**

| | |
|---|---|
| Potential new investors to the company | Financial statements as filed with the Registrar of Companies |
| Board of Directors | Balanced scorecard of the company |
| HM Revenue & Customs | Corporation tax return for the period |

Potential new investors would only have access to information available in the public domain, this would mainly be financial statements filed at Companies House. Share prospectus information may also be available for new listings, but this isn't an option here.

HMRC are concerned with the tax information available from the company, so although they would also require a copy of the financial statements, it would be most useful for them to use the Corporation Tax information which specifically shows any deductions or allowances as well.

The Board of Directors would require different information regarding the performance of the company, available to those within the company. The balanced scorecard would enable them to see what areas are performing well, and the Board could request further information, such as cash flows, however, this is likely to be covered already, in more detail in the scorecard report.

**(3 marks)**

**(c)**

| | |
|---|---|
| A payment was made to Tubs Supplies rather than Spa Supplies | Would not be detected |
| A cheque payment to Greenside & Co has not yet been banked by the supplier | Would be detected |
| A transposition error was made when recording a receipt in the cash book | Would be detected |
| A bank transfer was received by the bank but was omitted from the cash book | Would be detected |

Reconciliations are checks where staff ensure that two different sources of information agree, and that any differences are understood. So for a bank reconciliation, the differences between the bank statement and the cash book are investigated.

Therefore, payments made to the wrong customer would not be detected as the payments would tally on both sources.

The other errors would be detected as there would be a difference on the bank statement and the cash book.

**(4 marks)**

**(d)**

| | ✓ |
|---|---|
| A supervisory control | |
| A general IT control | |
| An authorisation control | ✓ |
| Segregation of duties | |

Malik is performing a review prior to adjusting journal entries being posted. He is therefore performing an authorisation control as his review is required before the next stage in the process (adjusting the cashbook) can be undertaken.

A supervisory control involves monitoring day-to-day accounting tasks, which is not Malik's role. A general IT control is one that protects the general computer environment which is some way relevant here as the reconciliation is performed in Excel and is emailed, but is not the control being undertaken by Malik. Segregation of duties in respect of the banking system would refer to the same member of staff not entering bank

transactions and performing the bank reconciliation. This is not the purpose of Malik's review.

**(2 mark)**

**(e)**

| | ✓ |
|---|---|
| The accounts receivable ledger only | ✓ |
| The accounts receivable ledger and the cash book | |
| The accounts receivable ledger and the general ledger | |
| The accounts receivable ledger, the general ledger and the cash book | |

A member of the credit control department needs access to the accounts receivable ledger only as they are interested in the amount owing from credit customers.

**(f)**  | Objectivity |

| You must raise the issue with Holly Turner |

| | ✓ |
|---|---|
| Reviewing new credit customer accounts for evidence that credit checks had been performed | |
| Ensuring that all orders are checked to current inventory levels before being accepted | ✓ |
| Comparing the amount of irrecoverable debts written off from one year to another | |
| Requiring that adjustments to standard selling process are authorised by an appropriate person | |

Ensuring that orders are checked to inventory levels before being accepted is a control within the sales system and helps to maintain customer goodwill, but it does not help to prevent and detect fraud.

# Task 2 (15 marks)

## (a)

An adverse sales variance suggests that the actual sales revenue achieved is lower than expected.

The sales budget may be set consistently so high that the hot tubs sales managers consider it to be unachievable. Rather than motivating them to try harder it will have the opposite effect, in that they will become demotivated and deterred from trying their best.

This is exacerbated if the sales budget includes items which are outside of the hot tub sales managers' control, for example if head office is responsible for selecting and purchasing the models of hot tubs available for sale.

The budget is set by head office, seemingly without input from the hot tub managers who are assessed on their ability to meet the budgets. This is likely to be a demotivating factor.

In terms of motivation, the sales budget should be set at a level that is challenging yet attainable. This will be more likely if restaurant managers are involved in the budget setting process and are only assessed on what they actually can affect, such as restaurant staff turnover, revenue generated per customer and food wastage.

Favourable variances in the consumables department budget suggests that the actual costs incurred are lower than expected.

If the variances in this department are consistently favourable, it may be that the consumables department manager is including budgetary slack in their cost estimates. This results in the consumables department not spending their full budget allocation and so there appear to be achieving favourable variances.

This is a problem because if all departments do this, the budgets will soon become unrealistic and meaningless. There will also be a temptation to spend up to the budget level when it is not necessary.

To improve this situation, the directors should discuss the importance of accurate budgeting with their managers and get them to buy in to its importance. Managers should be reassured that if they exceed spending for good reason compared to the a more accurate budget then they will not be penalised.

**(7 marks)**

**(b)**

Attractive potential rewards for staff: The rewards being offered by the performance related pay must be great enough to have an effect. If the potential rewards are small, then the motivating effect will be lost.

Relevant to the period: There should be a short timescale between the target being met and the reward being received, such as a financial year target, with the bonus being received within two to three months of the period end. This means that managers will have the reward in their sight and will try harder.

Control: The staff who have the performance related pay should be able to influence and control the factors affecting it. For example, a hot tubs sales manager should not be assessed on the quality of servicing. Instead, they could be assessed on an overall growth of 5% of revenue year on year, or the number of new customer contracts entered into in the year.

Long term aims of the company: Managers should be encouraged to buy in to the longer term goals of the company. This will improve their attitude to work generally and will also enhance the impact of the performance related pay.

In terms of goal congruence, there is a conflict between short-term and long-term decisions. The factors for performance related pay need to be assessed carefully:

- are the manager assessed on short term goals (such as the performance for that quarter only)?

- are the managers assessed on their product range only?

Revenue may be generated at the expense of profitability (such as by offering product discounts to attract customers, but affect longer profitability in the short term).

Do the aims of the managers meet with those of head office? Management need to ensure that they are working together as a group to attract customers. For example, a centrally organised discount will help the group as a whole by attracting customers to the products, but a manager deciding on discounts for their customers alone may impact other sales representatives or the brand as a whole.

A sales manager faces a conflict of interest between their personal interest (the performance-related pay) and what is right for the business. This may cause a self-interest threat to the manager's objectivity.

**(8 marks)**

## Task 3 (15 marks)

**(a)** **Note.** There are more weaknesses identified here than required, only five answers are required.

    **(i)** **Approved suppliers.** Whilst having a list of approved suppliers is positive for control puposes, the fact that the list is based on contacts Binny had from his previous roles rather than being based on price and reliability of suppliers is a weakness.

    **(ii)** **Approval of purchase orders.** Again, it is positive that there is an authorisation limit, but the amount of £10,000 seems far too high.

    **(iii)** **Binny reviews and accepts goods received.** The same person should not place orders and review and accept the goods received.

    **(iv)** **Danielle maintains standing data for suppliers and authorises BACS payments** which is a lack of segregation of duties.

    **(v)** **Danielle processes the BACS listing without review** which is a weakness as there should be a review and authorisation of the BACS listing before it it is processed.

    **(vi)** **Maisie inputs the invoices received without matching to purchase order.** Invoices should be matched to purchase orders before they are processed.

**(5 marks)**

**(b)**

| Weakness | Opportunity for fraud and error |
| --- | --- |
| Approved suppliers. | There is a risk that Binny is using suppliers who are not competitive in terms of their cost nor reliability which would be to the detriment of the company. Binny may be selecting the approved suppliers due to personal relationships or benefits he receives from those suppliers. |
| Approval of purchase orders | As the authorisation limit is set at £10,000 which seems to be a relatively high amount, there is a risk that Binny places orders below the authorisation limit that are not required for genuine business purposes. |

| Weakness | Opportunity for fraud and error |
|---|---|
| Binny reviews and accepts goods received | The lack of segregation of duties increases the risk that Binny can order goods that are not for genuine business purposes. |
| Danielle maintains standing data for suppliers and processes BACS payments | The lack of segregation of duties around the entering and amending of standing data and the processing of payments increases the risk that non-genuine suppliers are paid. |
| Danielle processes the BACS listing without review | Processing the BACS listing without review increases the risk that there are payments included on the listing that are not supported by purchase invoices. |
| Maisie inputs the invoices received without matching to purchase order | Maisie is accepting invoices without matching them to purchase orders and goods received notes. There is a risk that invoices are not for genuine orders and/or that invoices are not paid on a timely basis for goods received. |

**(10 marks)**

## Task 4 (15 marks)

**(a)** If both saunas and steam rooms are sold, the forecast revenue is £78,800 with a gross profit of £21,900 and a gross profit margin of 28%. The profit from operations will be £12,930 and the operating profit margin will be 16%. Selling both saunas and steam rooms is considered potentially risky and therefore we must consider the equivalent information if only the saunas or only the steam rooms are sold.

If only the saunas are sold, the forecasts for the year ending 31 December 20X3 is:

| | Saunas | Notes |
|---|---|---|
| Sales units | 25 | 20 saunas + 50% of steam room customers |
| | £ | |
| Revenue | 59,000 | At average price of £2,360 |
| Purchase of goods for resale | 25,245 | Average cost for units 1-20 is £1,020 <br> For units 21-25 is £969 |
| Labour costs | 13,125 | Variable therefore increases per unit sold |
| Other cost of sales | 2,000 | Fixed |
| Gross profit | 18,630 | 32% |
| Sales and distribution costs | 5,900 | Variable therefore increases per unit sold |
| Administration costs | 500 | Fixed |
| Profit from operations | 11,960 | 20% |

Based on the financial information provided, selling only the saunas would result in a higher gross profit margin (an increase of 3%) and an improved operating profit margin (an increase of 1%). The working capital cycle may be improved slightly if only saunas are sold as expenses, which are paid more quickly than receivables are collected, are lower.

**(8 marks)**

**(b)** In addition to the financial information provided, the directors of Holly's Hot Tubs Ltd should consider the following:

- The saunas are locally supplied. This may be attractive to customers who will be positive about the retention/creation of jobs in the local area and the low delivery miles for the products which is positive for the environment. This contrasts with the steam rooms which are sourced from a foreign supplier.

- There may be problems with continuity of supply from a foreign supplier if there are changes to legislation or other barriers to delivery of the products

- The steam rooms are not fixed price and will be subject to exchange rate movements which increases the risk that the cost of purchases will increase and margins will reduce

- The saunas are manufactured using sustainable wood whereas the steam rooms use non-recycled plastic. The company's environmental stance is not known, but there is a general consumer interest in more environmentally friendly products.

- The supplier of the saunas has an excellent reputation for quality and therefore there is less scope for follow up repairs being required or for negative customer reviews being left on social media

- It is not clear how the forecast information has been prepared, particularly the assumption that 50% of the forecast sales of saunas or steam rooms would transfer to the other product. Expert research and marketing advice would be required.

- The skill set is similar for both saunas and steam rooms, but it is not clear whether that skill set exists within the current staff.

**(7 marks)**

## Task 5 (20 marks)

**(a)**

| Holly's Hot Tubs Ltd Scorecard | Year ended 31 October 20X2 | Year ended 31 October 20X1 |
|---|---|---|
| **Profitability and working capital ratios** | | |
| Gross profit % | 41% | 50% |
| Operating profit % (W) | 2% | 16% |
| Return on capital employed % | 10% | 117% |
| Gearing (W) | 43% | 6% |
| Current ratio | 2.8:1 | 1.8:1 |
| Receivables collection period (W) | 54 Days | 0 Days |
| Payables payment period (use cost of sales) | 61 Days | 74 Days |
| Inventory holding period (W) | 66 Days | 49 Days |
| Working capital cycle (W) | 59 Days | (25) Days |

**(5 marks)**

**Workings**

| | Year ended 31 October 20X2 £000 |
|---|---|
| **Operating profit**<br>Operating profit/revenue × 100% | 33,694 / 1,684,720 × 100%<br>= 2% |
| **Gearing**<br>Debt/(debt + equity) × 100% | 148,000 / (148,000 + 193,259) × 100%<br>= 43% |
| **Receivables collection period**<br>Trade receivables/revenue × 365 | 247,600 / 1,684,720 × 365<br>=54 days |
| **Inventory holding period**<br>Inventory/cost of sales × 365 | 178,425 / 993,985 × 365<br>= 66 days |
| **Working capital cycle**<br>Inventory days + receivables days - payables days | (54 days + 66 days - 61 days)<br>= 59 days |

**(b)  Profitability**

| | ✓ |
|---|---|
| The gross profit has decreased due to a penalty paid for early termination of the rental of the head office. | |
| Operating profit has decreased due to the finance cost incurred on the loan. | |
| Gross profit has decreased due to the 10% reduction in selling prices. | ✓ |

Gross profit is a measure of revenue and the cost of sales.  A decrease in gross profit can be directly attributed to the decrease in selling prices.

A penalty for early termination of the head office rental is an operating cost and would not impact on gross profit.  Finance costs are not relevant for gross profit or operating profit.

**(2 marks)**

## Gearing

|  | ✓ |
| --- | --- |
| The increased gearing ratio is due to the fall in cash and cash equivalents in 20X2 |  |
| The increased gearing ratio is due to the bank loan taken out in 20X2 | ✓ |
| The increased gearing ratio is due to the additional interest costs incurred in 20X2 |  |

Gearing is directly impacted by debt, being the bank loan, and equity which is represented by the share capital and retained earnings. Cash and cash equivalents is not relevant for the purposes of calculating gearing.

**(2 marks)**

## Liquidity

|  | ✓ |
| --- | --- |
| Liquidity has improved in 20X2 due to the existence of trade receivables |  |
| An increased current ratio indicates that more cash is available to the company |  |
| The faster payment of trade payables contributes to the decreased cash and cash equivalents balance | ✓ |

The decrease in cash and cash equivalents can be attributed to (i) the increase in the collection period for trade receivables and (ii) the decrease in the length of time it takes to pay trade payables. An increased current ratio does not necessarily mean more cash is available, it simply means that current assets have increased relative to current liabilities.

**(2 marks)**

## Working capital

| | ✓ |
|---|---|
| The lengthening inventory holding period indicates that the company is finding it easier to sell its products | |
| The decreasing trade payables payment period has a positive impact on working capital | |
| The increasing trade receivables collection period has a negative impact on working capital | ✓ |

An increase in trade receivables means it takes longer to convert sales to cash. This has a negative impact on working capital, particularly where the collection period is longer than the payables payment period. A lengthening inventory holding period means it is taking longer for the company to sell its products.

**(2 marks)**

## Overall performance

| | ✓ |
|---|---|
| The financial statements show that the company paid a dividend in the year ended 31 October 20X1 | |
| The financial statements show that a loan was obtained for the purposes of working capital in the year ended 31 October 20X2 | ✓ |
| The financial statements show that the company is less risky at 31 October 20X2 than in the prior year | |

The financial statements do not indicate that a dividend was paid in either year as the increase in retained earnings is equal to the profit for the year. There has been no increase in non-current assets relating to the loan obtained which indicates that it was provided for working capital purposes. Overall, the existence of the large bank loan and the decrease in cash and equivalents increases the risk of the company at 31 October 20X2.

**(2 marks)**

## Task 6 (15 marks)

**(a)** The current payroll module was intended for 20 employees and Holly's Hot Tubs Ltd currently has 36 employees. The current module may therefore not have adequate capacity for the number of employees which increases the risk that the information prepared by the system would be inaccurate.

- The errors in calculating the statutory deductions indicate that the existing system is not reliable. As statutory deductions are reported to HMRC, there is a risk of penalties and fines if the deductions are not correct, as well as negative implications for staff morale.

- The payroll manager was appointed in May 20X2. The change to staffing raises some concerns as to whether they have the necessary skills and experience to undertake the role and whether they are applying the internal controls in the manner intended.

The regular monitoring of controls is essential otherwise there is a risk that the controls will not be adhered to by staff. Without monitoring of controls, there is an additional risk of fraud going undetected or errors being missed.

**(6 marks)**

**(b)** **Note.** There are more weaknesses identified here than required, only three answers are required.

| Weakness | Suitable improvement |
|---|---|
| Some deductions are manually calculated by the payroll manager | A fully automated system should be implemented which calculate all statutory and other deductions automatically. The deductions that are automatically calculated should be subject to review by the payroll manager to ensure they are accurate. |
| Niels is responsible for adding new employees and amending standing data | There should be segregation of duties, ideally with new employees added to the system by human resources and any amendments to the standing data should be reviewed and authorised by an appropriate level of management before it is processed. |

| Weakness | Suitable improvement |
| --- | --- |
| Employee time is assumed to be a standard 35 hours or 16 hours unless advised otherwise | Positive confirmation of the number of hours worked for each employee in each month should be received from the relevant managers. Niels should follow up on any non-replies before payment is processed. |
| The employees' managers advise whether overtime is worked on an evening or weekend | A formal time recording system which is entered by the employee and reviewed by the manager prior to being passed to the payroll department. |
| There is no review of the payroll listing prior to payments being processed. | The payroll listing should be reviewed by an appropriate level of management prior to being processed for payment. |

**(9 marks)**